MURDER & MAYHEM IN COEUR D'ALENE AND THE SILVER VALLEY

MURDER & MAYHEM IN COEUR D'ALENE AND THE SILVER VALLEY

DEBORAH CUYLE

THE History PRESS

Published by The History Press
Charleston, SC
www.historypress.com

First published 2022

Manufactured in the United States

ISBN 9781467149136

Library of Congress Control Number: 2022935428

Notice: The information in this book is true and complete to the best of our knowledge. It is offered without guarantee on the part of the author or The History Press. The author and The History Press disclaim all liability in connection with the use of this book.

I dedicate this book to everyone who loves Coeur d'Alene as much as I do! It's also dedicated to everyone who believes Idaho is as beautiful as I do. I dedicate this book to all the Idaho history aficionados out there; I hope our paths cross someday if they haven't already.

I also dedicate this book to all the police officers in Coeur d'Alene—from yesteryear as well as today. Your job is a tough one, and you do not receive enough appreciation for all you do to keep the beautiful city safe.

As always, I dedicate this book to my mom, Roxie, who always believed I could do anything I set up my mind to do. She was seldom wrong.

CONTENTS

PREFACE

I hope readers will enjoy immersing themselves in the shocking history of old Coeur d'Alene. With all my books, I try to incorporate as many historical facts, full names and dates as possible for each story. I feel this brings people to life and makes learning about the town more interesting. Many of my readers tell me they really enjoy learning about their town's history while reading about the local pioneers—their personal troubles, fears and accomplishments. With these true stories about early Coeur d'Alene, I hope to resurrect many of the local citizens, sneaky criminals and vigilantes, ladies of the night, barkeeps, hotel owners, bankers, politicians (and everyone in between). Otherwise, some of these people would have gone through their lives leaving no memories of themselves at all, except maybe a tombstone or an unmarked grave.

These true tales all occurred in the city of Coeur d'Alene or in the nearby towns. Other accounts are about people who only came through the Coeur d'Alenes in their travels, but they are such fascinating parts of the history of north Idaho, it would be a shame not to include them in this book.

I currently live in the Coeur d'Alene region and have fallen in love with it, so this book hits home with me. I have a great interest and extreme respect for the early pioneers, combined with a personal fascination for local history and old buildings. I love reading about the first settlers of a town—everyone from the Native tribes to the soldiers, immigrants and shopkeepers.

It is fun to walk the same streets today that early settlers once walked and think about how it was back in the old days.

When I look at time-worn brick buildings or century-old hardwood floors, I try to imagine the thousands of people who once visited these buildings. I think of the strong horses that once pulled wagons and goods down the streets. I think of the gunslingers and outlaws, the bartenders and shopkeepers—all of them living their lives and going about their business just as we all do today. I would have loved to have been alive back in the late 1800s.

Many of the stories in this book were pulled from old newspapers, recapturing early Coeur d'Alene's fascinating history and unique characters. The book is not intended to be a nonfiction project, because even after hundreds of hours hunched over, reading and researching articles, I still found conflicting dates and inconsistent historic details. So please take it for what it is and just enjoy the read. This is ultimately a book of the many mischievous and wild people and the interesting history of early Coeur d'Alene and the nearby towns nestled in the north Idaho territory.

I have been researching the area and its history for a number of years now, and the same familiar names pop up time after time as I review newspaper articles and stories about the goings-on in town—everything from robberies to murders, illnesses and marriages.

One of my favorite and fun stories is that of the local dog races in Coeur d'Alene. Citizens would enter their hounds, and frantic races would ensue down Sherman Avenue. Ed Cyr and his brother Gene started the somewhat unusual tradition. Pinky Palmerton's dad, who felt he deserved to win one year, attached a hot dog to the end of a long stick, thinking this would encourage his dog to run faster and win the race. Unfortunately, the hot dog did nothing more than start a hysterical dog fight among the contestants.

When scouring through reports and newspapers, sometimes the only remaining evidence of their existence at all is through their printed advertisements in the local newspapers. In legal trouble? Robert McFarland was the local attorney one would seek. Medical troubles? M.J. Libbel was a doctor and surgeon who had his practice on Fourth Street near the old city hall. Need a haircut or shave? F.E. Armstrong was the man to go to for a spruce up, with his barbershop situated next to the Miller Brothers Drug Store. A man named Chew Lee could wash your laundry, and if you needed a smoke, you could stop by G.E. Reynold's Cigar and Smoke Shop.

Although I have been unable to find any photographs of many of these individuals, I can picture them in my mind. I can visualize the rugged deputy sheriffs and night watchmen as they walk their beats, cracking down on bootleggers, robbers, prostitutes and drunks. I can hear the chime of the doorbell in my head as I think about the owners of the local shops preparing for the day, customers walking into their stores to buy their wares. I sympathize with the saloon owners and bartenders as they struggled with the day-to-day operations and headaches of running a public house and dealing with the constant array of disorderly customers. I applaud the hardworking hotel proprietors who often had to deal with unpleasant and unwanted situations, such as murder, suicide, arson and theft.

The strange and horrific (yet typical) events that occurred in Coeur d'Alene and the Silver Valley were not that uncommon at all compared to everywhere else. The only difference was that this area of northern Idaho held such extreme beauty, it was easy to turn a blind eye to any negative or uninvited situations.

Why observe the desperate and unfortunate women working in bawdy houses or the drunken and angry men stumbling out of a saloon when one could enjoy the view the beautiful blue lakes and picturesque Bitterroot Mountains?

But the beautiful city of Coeur d'Alene was a dangerous and menacing place in its early years.

The police were ever watchful of criminals and villains. Bar owners had to constantly protect their businesses and card games from unruly patrons and bandits. The desolate working girls employed in local houses of ill repute were shunned by society and were often suicidal or diseased. As the city grew, the reports of crimes grew with it. Murders, mysteries, kidnappings, robberies and more occupied the streets of early Coeur d'Alene and the nearby towns.

Let's step back one hundred years and immerse ourselves in Coeur d'Alene's dark, fascinating and sordid history, shall we?

ACKNOWLEDGEMENTS

There are many people to thank for this endeavor, and without their help and guidance, this book would not have been possible. My wonderful editor, Artie Crisp, has been such a pleasure to work with on my Coeur d'Alene books, along with all of the other incredible people at Arcadia Publishing and The History Press. Their mission to promote local history is passionate and infectious, and I am blessed to create my many books with them! Their dedication to recording local history is nothing less than amazing, and without them, many books would never be written.

My appreciation is extended to all those individuals who took the time to share local records and documents with me. Without them, this book would not have the extra flair that I love so much.

And as always, I want to thank every single person who does what they can to preserve history, whether it is volunteering at the local historical society, maintaining old cemeteries and gravestones that would otherwise be neglected or simply researching their private genealogy through sites like Ancestry.com. In this fast-paced and high-tech world, the past can unfortunately be easily forgotten, and every effort to maintain and record valuable data, photographs, diaries, documents and records is of the utmost importance for future generations.

I also want to thank my followers and friends who have supported my craft all these years.

And of course, I want to thank my cat, Lily, for taking the time to walk across my keyboard right before I get a chance to save my work. She is always so helpful!

INTRODUCTION

The boys with their feet on the desks know that the easiest murder case in the world to break is the one somebody tried to get very cute with; the one that really bothers them is the murder somebody only thought of two minutes before he pulled it off.
—Raymond Chandler

Coeur d'Alene—a city as beautiful today as it was in the late 1800s, when it mesmerized people from all over the United States. What more could they ask for? A picturesque city situated next to a deep, crystal-blue lake and gorgeous mountainsides—perfection!

But the town's dark history is not all roses and laughter. It contains tales of desperate gamblers, greedy prostitutes and fraught prospectors who did everything they could to secure their own future—sometimes at any cost. If the walls could talk in the buildings that still stand in Coeur d'Alene, they would whisper dark tales of hushed murders, illegal gambling, excessive drinking, corrupt politicians and labor disputes that sometimes led to cold-blooded murder.

Such interesting characters emerge, such as former Wallace mayor Herman Rossi, who killed a man in cold blood one dark night in the lobby of the Samuel's Hotel (in front of many witnesses) yet was magically acquitted on all charges.

Learn about the soiled doves who worked in the many bordellos and cribs that lined the back streets near the muddy banks of the Coeur d'Alene River. Some of these houses of prostitution were extremely profitable and

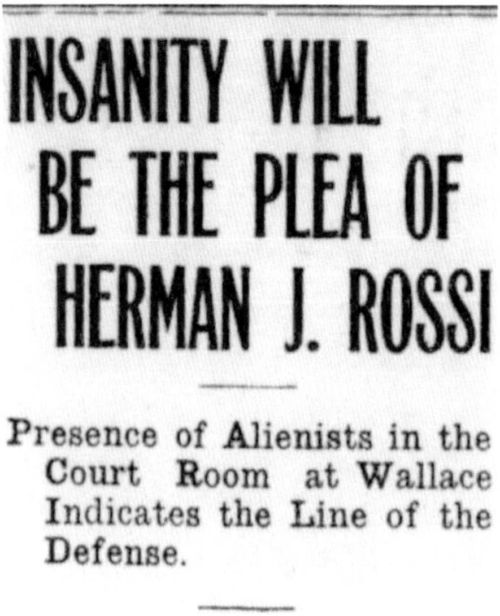

INSANITY WILL BE THE PLEA OF HERMAN J. ROSSI

Presence of Alienists in the Court Room at Wallace Indicates the Line of the Defense.

Left: Herman Rossi's lawyer pushed the temporary insanity plea for the murder of Gabe Dahlquist. *From the* Evening Capital News, *October 6, 1916.*

Right: Wyatt Earp spent a year in the Coeur d'Alenes making money off the working miners. He was once the deputy sheriff of Eagle City, Idaho, near Murray. *From Wikipedia.*

supported the local community, while the seedy ones were plagued by thievery, greed and spur-of-the-moment murders. Many soldiers who visited the bordellos for a night of fun never returned to their posts at Fort Sherman the next morning. They simply disappeared into the dark underworld of gambling, drinking and dishonest women—some victims were personally hastily buried by Coeur d'Alene's ruthless crime monster Fatty Carroll.

Silver mining and land claim disputes often lead to shoot-outs and "accidental" deaths, and most murders were never even reported to the police. Other ongoing conflicts led to calculated homicides, such as the bomb that instantly killed Idaho's governor Frank Steunenberg. He had recently (and fatally) promised to "punish and totally eradicate criminals who for years had been committing murders."

Even the legendary Wyatt Earp lived in the Coeur d'Alene territory for a short time in 1884. Following a gold rush that never arrived, the Wyatt clan decided to make the most of it and set up shop. In a small town called Eagle City (near the town of Murray), the Wyatt brothers purchased a large circus-style tent and called it the White Elephant Saloon. They advertised their business as "the largest and finest saloon in the Coeur d'Alenes!"

They made a good living providing whiskey to thirsty miners and loggers. They provided female dancers and gambling for entertainment.

That spring, two groups of men began bickering over a property dispute, and the bullets began to fly. Over fifty shots were fired back and forth between the two groups. Wyatt and his brother Jim calmly sauntered in between the angry mob—bullets whizzing overhead—and tried to pacify the men. The men agreed to talk out their differences, and luckily, no one was killed. The gunslinging Wyatt Earp soon became the deputy sheriff of Kootenai County.

But his recklessness soon brewed trouble in the mountains. Wyatt reportedly began claim jumping against a local man named Andrew Prichard. Earp soon found himself in trouble with the law and was rumored to have been scheduled to be hanged in Murray, Idaho. Wyatt and his family quickly moved out of town in the dark of the night, still owing over three dollars in back taxes. That winter, it is documented that the Earps landed in New Mexico Territory, far away from the Coeur d'Alene troubles.

As Coeur d'Alene spiraled out of control, the demand for law and order escalated.

These and many other stories of Coeur d'Alene's old-fashioned debauchery and sinners who lurked in its dark corners are within these pages.

Sit a while and immerse yourself in the sordid (yet fascinating) past of beautiful Coeur d'Alene.

1
COEUR D'ALENE MURDERS

A murderer is regarded by the conventional world as something almost monstrous, but a murderer to himself is only an ordinary man. It is only if the murderer is a good man that he can be regarded as monstrous.
—Graham Greene

Surprisingly, there were many murders and related crimes in Coeur d'Alene in its early years. Some unruly men traveled to the city for the sole purpose of finding easy targets to rob.

When the city was in its infancy in 1883, there were only a handful of settlers in the area. Robert Cocheran was a miner working the mountains in search of treasures. The Turners had a farm in town. Fatty Carroll had a place on the Spokane River and a dance hall over by the mill that was considered the "toughest joint in history!" Tony Tubb had the Hotel d'Landing and a ranch where the Coeur d'Alene Lumber Company would sit in the future. W.H. McLaughlin and John Clinton had houses in town along with a few others. The following year, there were tents galore scattered all around the new city.

In 1902, the Fort Sherman Lumber Company sprouted up near the old Fatty Carrol place. It was erected on seventy-plus acres, with a half mile of riverfront acreage. It could churn out an incredible forty thousand feet of lumber in just ten hours. The lumber mill was built on a flat parcel where the Riverside Saloon once stood.

An unidentified policeman dressed in a uniform around 1873. *C.M. Bell, photographer, Library of Congress, no. 2016712631.*

The small town of Coeur d'Alene was rocking and buzzing with all kinds of activity.

It is a shame to read about so many murders, with the public facts being nothing more than a few written sentences in the local papers. It seems as though it was fairly common to have no follow-up investigation, no criminal convictions and sadly no resolution for the family members and friends.

In 1904, a young Coeur d'Alene boy, Paul Graff, was accidentally shot in the stomach and killed by night watchman James Murphy. He was in his uncle's office off the Sunset Brewery building in the wee hours of the morning for unknown reasons, and the officer mistook him for a robber. Murphy shot him through the window, thinking he was a burglar. Not much more was ever found out about poor Paul or whatever came of the incident.

Unfortunately, a life was tragically taken, and without modern-day forensic science to help the police catch the killer, many homicides went unsolved. Astonishingly, some crimes were unraveled by such simple clues as an unusual button found under a bed in a hotel room or a few odd coins pawned off at a bar.

In the early 1900s, horse stealing was a serious crime, one that could lead to murder. A man could go to jail for two to seven years for stealing another man's horse. Why? It was a fact that if a man was traveling out on the open range and was left there without his horse, he could and would probably die. Homesteaders depended on their horses, mules and cattle to survive. Unfortunately, there were not enough United States Marshals to deal with all the horse theft, so law-abiding men formed their own group to ward off equine theft and called themselves the Horse Thief Association. When horse and cattle thieves were captured, it was these men (not the marshals) who were in charge of any hangings that were to be done. Big, strong trees soon came to be known as "hanging trees" and became popular in the region as well as all over the United States.

Some of the more notorious horse thieves in the Coeur d'Alenes were brothers Theodore and William Bishop, William Boultier and E.W. Wheeler. In May 1909, they stole six horses from O.A. Roberts; the horses were valued at $350. The horses were secretly corralled at the nearby

Bishop Farm. But a law-abiding man named S.R. Dishman caught wind that the men had plans to cross the Montana border with the stolen horses, so he notified both the local sheriff and the Horse Thief Association.

When the criminals were captured, they were hanged from a nearby and handy strong tree.

1883: James "Fatty" Carroll: Coeur d'Alene's First Serial Killer?

Some people believe Coeur d'Alene's ruthless "Fatty" never existed and was simply a figment of several writers' imaginations over the years.

But nothing could be further from the truth.

Around 1883, Carroll was one of the few original residents in the Coeur d'Alene area, located near Fort Sherman when it as nothing more than a small group of people. He lived among Robert Cocheran, the Turner family and Tony Tubbs. Two men, Clafin and Evans, had a saloon called the Fashion on the corner opposite Ford's saloon.

On June 1, 1901, the *Coeur d'Alene Press* stated that most locals considered Fatty the "king of Coeur d'Alene." His businesses flourished during the late 1880s in the area and was classified as one of the toughest joints in the county. Coeur d'Alene itself was known as one of the hardest towns between Portland, Oregon, and St. Paul, Missouri.

Some suggest Fatty's real name was Jim Metzger or James Carroll, among other aliases.

Fatty owned and ran a dance hall near the Spokane River, and he lived above it. It was rumored that he had a special trapdoor built over the river, and if you were ushered into that room, you did not come out alive.

Your bloody corpse was simply dropped into the icy, cold river to float downstream.

James "Fatty" Carroll owned several businesses over the course of several decades in Coeur d'Alene. Snippets about Fatty were often written in the Coeur d'Alene newspapers. People speculated that Fatty had his very own private cemetery located somewhere on his property in Coeur d'Alene.

Although he was productive in business and profits, it appears he lacked social skills and patience. It was said that if Fatty didn't like you, you were not long for this world.

Around 1887, Fatty owned a store on the corner of Mullan and Fourth Streets in town simply called Carroll's Variety Store. It was located at the base of Tubb's Hill (now the area known as McEuen Park). His bartender was a gentleman named A.J. Coffman, and the pianist was James C. Smythe. This was the spot to go to if one wanted to partake in gambling, whoring and drinking. Fatty offered all three services at a good price.

Fatty owned another cat house on the corner of Fourth Street and Sherman Avenue.

He forced his working girls to sometimes rob the men who came looking for a good time. If they resisted being robbed, Fatty would take care of them.

In 1887, three innocent soldiers went into town looking to have some fun. The next morning, during roll call, they never responded and were never seen again.

On February 12 that same year, a pay back to Fatty may have been played. That cold evening, Fatty Carroll's dance hall/variety store caught fire. Two people tragically died—a female worker named Lottie Haines and a man known only as "Uncle John." Supposedly, a lamp caught fire, and the two-story building was burned to the ground within minutes.

The bartender, Andrew J. Coffman, was working at the time and gave the *Idaho Semi-Weekly World* his version of the story:

> *Mr. Jas. Carroll, the proprietor, was down the river a couple miles looking after affairs at his logging camp at the time and did not get back before a moment the building fell in. Someone above called, "Fire!" And a few seconds later, a man named Haines or Harris jumped out of the window from the upper story. It seems that a burning lamp on a table exploded, the noise being distinctly heard, and the hallway was immediately filled with smoke. A woman named Lottie Haines, who was in bed upstairs, fainted, and Haines or Harris endeavored to carry her to the window in order to let her down, but the flames and smoke nearly suffocated him, he was compelled to abandon the woman, who was burned up, the* [her] *charred trunk being found in the ashes of the building. An old man known as "Uncle John" dropped dead from heart disease while endeavoring to save his property.*

Fatty wasn't the only scrappy Carroll. The *Spokane Falls Review* reported on July 21, 1887, that Fatty Carroll's "woman" (no name was given) shot and severely injured another dancer at Fatty's dance hall in Coeur d'Alene where he was the proprietor. The victim suffered a bullet hole in her thigh but survived. The victim's name was also not given. It seems as though violence ran in the blood of the Carrolls.

In October 1897, Fatty found himself in front of Judge Will on assault and battery charges. One of his tenants, a shoemaker named Bade Grunch, threatened Fatty. It wasn't long before Grunch took back his statement, stating that he and Fatty had "worked things out."

More likely, if Grunch wanted to keep on this side of the grass or to keep himself from floating in the river, he would retract the claim and get about his merry way.

Not much can be found about Fatty after this incident. Where did Fatty go? Did he sense trouble brewing and his problems catching up with him?

In the summer of 1901, the Coeur d'Alene Lumber Company was developing on the site of the old opera house in town. The workers soon found what was left of a body. Part of the skull, lower jaw, a few larger bones and several ribs were all that was left of the victim. Although foul play was suspected, there was really no way of knowing who the deceased was.

In 1902, the Fort Sherman Lumber Company purchased Fatty's old farm of seventy acres to build a lumber mill on the spot near the river. The next few years were when things got weird.

Fatty also owned a former dive near Fort Sherman, where soldiers could get drunk and mysteriously disappear. When men began excavating in 1903 at the old site for the Coeur d'Alene and Spokane Railway Company, seven corpses were unearthed.

The workers stopped digging, and the police were called in to investigate. The officers searched an area of land approximately thirty by thirty feet. More skeletons were found.

Later that year, while workers were grading for the new Coeur d'Alene Lumber Company, two decayed bodies were found crammed into a rotting wooden box. This parcel was the exact spot where one of Fatty Carroll's businesses once stood.

Where Carroll's Variety Store once stood, near Sherman Avenue by the train station, more skeletons were found.

In September 1903, another grisly discovery was made. Men who were digging for the new electric line on Mullan Road near Fort Sherman and Coeur d'Alene stumbled across another corpse.

In the fall of 1903, Fatty was again squirming in front of a judge. He and a man named John W. Garton got into a fight at the Crystal Saloon in Spokane on the corner of Main and Division Streets. The two men apparently got into a brawl inside the saloon, and Garton proceeded to take Fatty down to the ground. Garton must have been a very brave (or very stupid) man. Garton had Fatty on the floor in front of the bar, his boot crushing down on Fatty's face.

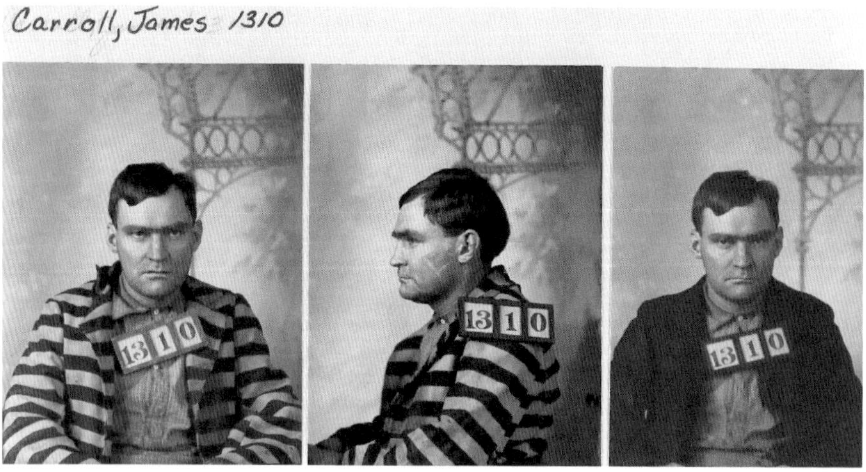

Possibly the mug shot of Coeur d'Alene's notorious killer "Fatty Carroll," whose real name was James Carroll. He received his facial scar in a bar fight. *Courtesy of the Idaho State Penitentiary and Ancestry.*

Both were promptly arrested for disorderly conduct. Fatty's face and head were bandaged from the bottom of his chin all the way to the top if his head.

Then, when excavating began for Dr. Scallion's Block on the corner of Fourth Street and Sherman Avenue, another body in a box was uncovered.

In 1906, workers began prepping the site for the new Wilson's Pharmacy. This location is where Fatty once owned a busy cat house where men were known to go missing. Hidden down in the dark basement, the workers found the bodies of three Natives and five soldiers.

The world will never know where Fatty disappeared to before the discovery of all the bodies or if he found himself in a wooden box, buried somewhere under a few feet of earth in Coeur d'Alene.

It seems as though Fatty no longer hung out in Coeur d'Alene for one reason or another.

1899: CORYELL KILLS OLESON, MISTAKES HIM FOR A DOG

The morning of May 15, 1899, started out much the same as any other day on the family farm in the Elk Mountain area of Kootenai County near Coeur d'Alene. Chores were to be done, fences had to be mended and animals had to be fed.

But this particular day would end in a horrible tragedy for the Oleson family. By early evening, Peter Oleson, aged seventy years, would be pronounced dead. He was murdered by his neighbor's worker N.H. Coryell, who shot him with a .32-40 Winchester rifle from a distance.

When the police questioned Coryell about the killing, he did not deny it; instead, he offered that he thought he had actually shot the Oleson family's dog that was chasing his boss's cattle.

When the police investigated the murder, they questioned Oscar Oleson, Peter's son. He testified in court that the day of the murder, he was fixing a fence when he heard his father holler for him. Three times the old man yelled across the field one hundred yards away for his son. Running toward the sound of his father's distressed cries for help, the boy found his dad near death. It was nearly nightfall, around 7:30 p.m., when the shots were fired. The horrified Oscar ran and told his mom about the incident, and she immediately ran to her husband's side.

Next, the frightened boy ran to the neighbor's house, the Hutton's farm, to try to get help, but (unknown to him) it was already too late. The Huttons were not home.

His father had passed away from the bullet wound while he was running to get help. He would never speak to his father again.

The distressed Mrs. Mary Oleson sat next to her bleeding husband. He asked where Oscar was. The man looked into his wife's eyes and said, "I am dying pretty soon." His wife asked him if he knew who shot him, but his words were muffled and quiet.

Just minutes later, Mr. Oleson was dead.

The neighbors gathered together and hurried to the Oleson ranch, where they found Mr. Oleson lying in his blood, the grieving family by his side. They carried his body into the house.

Later that night, Mr. Chas Wells and Mr. J.M. Hutton cautiously visited the Oleson farm. Mr. Wells asked Oscar about his father, "He was shot? Is he going to be all right?"

Angry and confused, the boy responded, "Yes, he was shot, and now he is dead! Do you know who done it?"

Wells turned and asked Hutton if he knew who had shot Mr. Oleson. Without hesitation, he replied, "Yes, I do…it was Coryell."

"How do you know?" inquired Wells.

"Because he told me," said Hutton. He also disclosed that Coryell was going to stay the night at another neighbor's farm, the Boots's farm. Coryell had been hired to watch and tend to Boots's cattle for the summer.

A mug shot of N.H. Coryell, who murdered a man because his dog was chasing cattle. *Courtesy of the Idaho State Penitentiary and Ancestry.*

The men discussed what they had heard Coryell tell them many times: "If he ever saw a man chasing cattle with a dog, he would just as soon shoot the man as the dog." I guess he finally kept his promise.

On May 24, Coryell was rounded up, arrested and questioned in the courtroom.

He admitted to hunting down and shooting at the Oleson's dog in the dark of night. After he fired the gun, he heard the cries coming from the direction of his shot and realized he had accidentally hit a man, not a dog.

The defense attorney asked him about this. "When you heard someone holler in the distance, why did you not immediately go to their assistance?"

"Well, Sir, I was so wild, I did not know what to do. I knew that I had hit someone."

"Did you know it was Mr. Oleson?"

"Yes, Sir, by the voice."

He told the court that he had returned to the Boots's farm then headed to the Hutton farm. He told Mr. Hutton that he had accidentally shot Oleson when he was trying to kill their dog. Mr. Hutton advised Coryell that he should go to the police and tell them what had happened.

So with that, Coryell and Hutton made their way to Mr. Carpenter's, the justice of the peace, house and told the story of the shooting.

On May 17, Coryell was released on an $800 bail. His trial was set for early December. Almost forty men were brought in to be jurors for the case. They were educated on the differences between murder in the first degree, murder in the second degree and manslaughter. Sheriff Fred Bradbury accompanied Coryell to the courtroom on December 6 for his trial. On December 21, the jury came to their decision.

"We the jury find the defendant, N.H. Coryell, guilty of the crime of manslaughter."

In 1899, manslaughter was described as:

> *The unlawful killing of a human being without malice. It is of two kinds; 1. Voluntary—upon a sudden quarrel or heat of passion and 2. Involuntary—in the commission of an unlawful act not amounting to a felony; or in the commission of a lawful act which might produce death, in an unlawful manner, or without due caution or circumspection.*

Kootenai County Jail, Rathdrum.

The Kootenai County Jail, located in Rathdrum, held many prisoners over the years. *From the* Rathdrum Tribune, *July 31, 1908.*

On December 26, the day after Christmas, Coryell received his judgment. He would spend the next five years in the county jail in Rathdrum.

His parole regulations covered some interesting notes and rules for Coryell to follow:

> *He shall at all times abstain from the use of intoxicating drinks and narcotics, tobacco excepted, and from gambling in any form whatsoever, and from loitering in or about houses of ill fame, and saloons or resorts where liquor is sold or gambling carried on: also from carrying or using firearms or any other deadly weapon. He shall refrain from the commission of any crime and in every way conduct himself in a sober, industrious manner and avoid all vicious and evil associates.*

No further information can be found about the whereabouts of Coryell, but one thing is certain: a life was taken, a family was altered forever and a man wasted five years in jail—all because a dog was chasing some cattle.

1906: LaFenirer Kills Erb with a Shot Through the Penis

October 1906 was a bad time for two men in particular. What may have started out as an innocent night of drinking and gambling turned into nightmare. Denny LaFenirer (also LaFernirer or LaFerneie), Bert Erb and many others were hanging out in a local saloon called Hendershott's. While most of the men were just chatting, playing cards and drinking, tension was brewing between LaFenirer and Erb. At about 8:00 p.m., Erb (being in a good mood) decided to buy a round of drinks for the house. This made the hardworking men in the bar very happy indeed. Everyone cheered and gathered near the bar to await their free shot of whiskey—everyone except LaFenirer, who continued to just sit on a barrel and glare at Erb.

LaFenirer lagged back and slowly sipped on the whiskey he already had in his hand. After a few minutes, when the locals had gotten served their free drink and resumed what they were previously doing, LaFenirer slowly made his way to the bar. After a bit of heated talk, Erb put his hand on LaFenirer's shoulder. After a few more angry words, the two men began to scuffle. After a few shoves and more bad words, the grown men were rolling around the wood floor of Hendershott's like a couple of out-of-control kids.

LaFenirer yelled, "Stay away from me," but Erb didn't listen. LaFenirer quickly pulled out his gun, hoping this would convince Erb to get off him, but it didn't. No one in the bar even knew what the men were even arguing about. The other patrons just moved away to give the men more space to fight it out. Not everyone saw the gun hidden in LaFenirer's hand, or they probably would have gotten the heck out of there.

Next, the loud sounds erupted inside the saloon. *Boom! Boom! Boom! Boom! Boom!* Five ear-shattering gunshots were fired in rapid succession. Everyone froze. The two men lay in a heap on the bloody floor. Later, it was discovered that Erb only had a jack knife on him, and it had remained closed during the scuttle.

"Take him off me, boys. He got me!" yelled Erb. As the men put down their drinks and helped poor old Erb up off the floor, they noticed he was holding his stomach.

The shooter called to the men, "I have got him. Tell Mr. Hendershott to go get the doctor. He says I have got him in the guts!" cried LaFenirer.

Mr. Hendershott quickly summoned the doctor for help. As they were waiting for him to arrive, the patrons laid Erb on the poker table. He was bleeding badly, and the men all thought this was the end of Erb.

Strangely, Erb whispered, "Take off my shoes." A man nearby, Lewis, pulled one shoe from the dying man. Another man, Al Duckworth, who had known Erb for nine years, went to his side.

Whispers of "Al, they have got me," was all Erb could get out.

Soon, Dr. J.L. Rogers appeared with his physician's bag and ran over to where Erb was lying. It didn't look good, but Dr. Rogers did what he could until they got the man to the hospital.

Dr. Rogers stayed near Erb's side for four days, tending to his wounds.

Upon examination, Erb had received five gunshots in all; two in the stomach, one just left of his navel, one in his thigh and, unfortunately, one through his penis.

Infection began to set in, and soon, Erb had what was called peritonitis.

Erb remained alive for ninety-four long and painful hours. He died at 6:00 p.m. on October 24, 1906.

The murderer was moved to Rathdrum Jail on March 21, 1907, and a trial was completed for LaFenirer with eleven eyewitnesses telling the story of Erb's murder.

Prosecuting attorney Ezra Whitla filed no. 189, *State of Idaho v. Denny LaFenirer*, on December 11, 1906. The complaint was written with way too many herefores and thereins and therebys, but basically, the condensed version reads: "On the 20th day of October 1906, in Kootenai County, in the State of Idaho, Denny LaFenirer did then and there willfully, violently, feloniously and unlawfully with premeditated malicy shoot off and discharge at and upon the of one Bert Erb, a certain revolver, held and loaded with powder and ball."

Oddly, on December 27, 1907, over a year later, written and filed by C.H. Potts, attorney for the State of Idaho, was the final word on the matter: "The defendant has not been brought to final trial, absence of material witness for the state, whose attendance could not be secured. The trial would cause needless expense to Kootenai County, and the dismissal hereof would be in furtherance of justice."

The case against LaFenirer was dismissed by Judge Woods. Why? No further information has been found. Yet there must be more to the story.

1907–9: FLOATERS FOUND IN CDA LAKE

A series of murders occurred in Coeur d'Alene between 1907 and 1909 that seemed to be that of another local serial killer. The bodies of men were found floating in the lake near the city; their murders remain unsolved to this day.

On May 26, 1907, the bloated body of a man was found in the lake at 2:00 p.m. on the beach near Foster's place by Otis Edmond's. It was believed the body had actually been in the lake since April. Edmond quickly notified the undertaker Lemmer, who went to gather the body of the victim.

The police felt it was one of the two out of the three men who went boating on April 7: James Collins, J.R. Murray and William Christenson. Their boat was reported to have become unbalanced, and only Murray survived. Murray told officers that Collins and Christenson had tragically drowned. Collins's body was nowhere to be found. Christenson was a single twenty-two-year-old man who worked as a night cook at the Lakeview Café and Saloon in town. He had come to the city with his nephew August a few weeks earlier looking for some fun. He liked Coeur d'Alene so much he decided to stay. His body was identified by papers found in his pockets that survived the water damage. Was this truly a boating accident or foul play?

Two months later, on July 25, the tattered and bloated remains of James Collins finally appeared. Early that morning, a man saw them floating near the shore, about two miles away from Coeur d'Alene near H.A. Anderson's home. The grisly discovery left the man shaking. The coroner found a notebook with the name Jim Collins written on it inside the victim's clothing that verified his identity. There was also a poll tax receipt in his pocket with his name on it. The identity of the body was not really questioned, but the men's deaths were.

Strangely, Collins's body carried a handwritten suicide note that read:

> *My address is 13, Jim Collins, Milton House, Belfast, Ireland. I am tired of life, so I have finished my miserable existence. Farewell to friends and foe. Jim, 24, Jan. '07.*

Once notified, his saddened family in Ireland sent a telegram back to the telegraph office in Coeur d'Alene requesting that that his body be buried in Idaho. He was buried at Forest Cemetery at 221 South Fifth Street in Coeur d'Alene, plot D-01-20. The secret truth about his death—whether it be a suicide, murder or accident—went to his grave with him. The only man who lived through the tragic boating accident was sticking to his story.

When the only survivor, John R. Murray, was questioned again by authorities, he told his side of the tragic story once again:

> *We had been drinking in town all day, then we decided to take a boat out from the Coeur d'Alene Boat Livery around noon on the 3rd of April. Christenson was the most sober and also the only one skilled about being on the water, so he took control of the oars. We were headed to Kidd Island Bay (about ½ a mile east of Tubb's Point) in the boat when Christenson and Murray decided to switch sides. When I did this, I stepped on the gunwale (the narrow sides of the boat), which made the boat rock and immediately capsize, dumping all three of us into the water. We all struggled, but only I was able to hang onto the boat and stay afloat. Sadly, Christenson and Collins quickly drowned and sank to the bottom of the lake.*

The man who rescued Murray, Otis Edmonds (also Emmons or Redmond) told his version of the story from that fatal day:

> *I am the caretaker for the Foster home on the lake. My dog started barking at something in the water. I quickly grabbed my small boat and headed out to the direction of the scene. There, I found Murray hanging onto the overturned boat alone. I pulled Murray from the water and brought him back to shore. The two other men were nowhere to be found.*

But a detective might question a few facts from these stories told by Murray and Edmonds—they don't add up.

- Collins's "suicide" note stated he was twenty-four years old when he was recorded as being thirty-five. It is ridiculous to think the victim did not know his own age.
- Kidd Island Bay is located two and a half miles from the city of Coeur d'Alene and is not very wide. Why did Murray and Edmonds not stick around to at least try to look for Christenson and Collins? Christenson could have easily swam back to shore instead of treading water until he was so tired he drowned. And why did the other two men not also grab hold of the boat like Murray did to stay afloat? There is not a known strong current in the area or undertow.
- If Christenson was an "experienced" boatman and "accustomed to the water" (as Murray told reporters), why could he not swim? Also, wouldn't he know enough about boats to not step on the gunwale, which would obviously cause the boat to flip and capsize?
- Murray claimed they went boating on April 3, but the receipt and date of accident was the April 7. If you had been involved in a tragic accident in which two comrades drowned in front of your eyes, getting the date wrong seems odd.
- The most compelling evidence of foul play in this book is that if this was truly an accident, would Collins really have had time to write a suicide note before drowning? If Collins was truly as miserable and depressed as his note made it sound, why would he have gone out boating with friends?

Another very strange coincidence? Otis Edmonds (who originally rescued Murray on April 7) was also the person who found William Christenson's body later on May 26.

Murray was not a model citizen. While his friend Christenson was lying on a cold slab at the morgue, Murray was busying himself by trying to commit robbery. He broke into the room of Fred Woods at the Otterson Block building in Coeur d'Alene through a window. Woods was also a night bartender at the Lakeview Café and Saloon (curiously, Christenson also worked at the saloon). When Woods went to his room to retire after a long shift, he discovered his room had been ransacked. He had several old

John Murray became entangled in mysterious deaths in 1907. When he later stole old coins and bought a hamburger at the Hotel Idaho, police became suspicious. *From the* Coeur d'Alene Press, *October 31, 1906.*

and valuable coins hidden in his room, and they had been stolen. Woods immediately reported the theft to the policeman nearby, Officer Jackson.

When Jackson investigated the room, the only clue he could find was a single blue steel button found on the floor. The men realized the button did not come from any of Woods's clothing.

Officer Jackson began inquiring around town. Later that night, when Jackson talked to the bartender at the Central Saloon, he was told he had served a man some drinks—nothing unusual there. But what was unusual was that the man paid for the drinks with very old coins. Down a block or two a little later that night, the cook at a hamburger joint at the Hotel Idaho said he was also paid for a meal with old coins. The cook gave a quick description of the criminal to Jackson, and the officer was hot on the thief's trail.

As Jackson was searching for the criminal, he noticed a man nervously poke his head out from a hallway in a building on the Otterson Block of Sherman Street. When the man suspiciously took off running, Jackson quickly followed him up the stairs of the building. When the officer caught the stranger, he accused him of stealing the coins from Woods's room. Of course, Murray denied his guilt, but Jackson was not going to give up that easy. When he inspected Murray's pants, he noticed a single blue steel button was missing. When Jackson told Murray that a single blue steel button had been found on the floor of Woods's room, he quietly confessed to the crime. He told the officer that he had hidden the rest of the coins in a basket in the hallway. Jackson promptly took Murray off to jail.

Strangely, Woods did not want to prosecute Murray, but Chief McGovern did. It was later discovered that Murray's favorite stomping and drinking ground was the Lakeview Saloon and that he knew Woods from hanging out at the bar.

Then in 1908, another bloated body was found floating in the lake. This time, there was definitive evidence of foul play. In May, Captain Sam Avery of the log tugboat *Bessie* and its crew discovered a dead man's body in the water near the beach at Tubb's Point. The undertakers Lemmer and Gross were soon waiting at the shore to retrieve the body and take it back to the morgue. Within hours, a multitude of people were waiting to see if they could identify the poor victim.

What was known about the victim? The deceased was a larger, older man with gray hair and beard. He had been in the water for approximately five to ten days. A strange, square-shaped hole had been punched into his forehead and into his brain by an unknown object, possibly a pick hammer. His face was also bruised. He was missing his index finger on his left hand. He wore clothes similar to the kind a woodsman would wear.

Back at the morgue, several people felt sure they could identify who the murdered man was.

First possibility: Fred Hunter. A former boss named Bob Mann said he had gone missing about three weeks earlier, but Hunter did not have a beard when he went missing. He also stated that Hunter never lost a finger while employed by him. Other friends who knew Hunter for years felt he was missing a finger but could not recall which one. The motive? Hunter had been having trouble in town, and an unknown arsonist had visited his house, threatening to burn it down. Eventually, the arsonist was successful, and Hunter's place was burned down. Also, his neighbors did not like him and collectively agreed to do away with him. Another man, N.H. Gilman, was positive the body belonged to Hunter.

Second possibility: John Brady, a local timberman and miner who worked at a mine at Rose Lake who was missing. The motive? There was none. Brady had no known enemies, but it was reported that when he got drunk, he could get mean and ugly. I.T. Quaries who ran the Bandbox Saloon in Coeur d'Alene, felt it was Brady. Another man who had known Brady for a number of years, Robert Kerchivel, peered in on the victim and was convinced it was Brady. Kerchivel stated that he felt Brady was a peaceful man and had never seen him mean or drunk. Some suggested that Brady may have just got paid and that the motive was robbery.

Third possibility: Jake Hoover. This theory was soon dismissed, as several who viewed the body agreed it was not Jake Hoover.

Coroner Wenz conducted an autopsy of the dead man, and when he cut his skull open, he noted that the instrument used was sharp and that it was not a bullet. The skull had also been fractured by a blow to the head—but by what? The hole in the forehead was square in shape, probably, Wenz deduced, caused by a handpick.

Miners were known to carry and use handpicks. Did a fellow miner kill this person? If it was Brady, who would have wanted to kill him?

More Floaters Are Found in Lake Coeur d'Alene

On May 9, 1908, another body of a dead man was found floating in the Coeur d'Alene River near downtown. The deceased had suffered extensive wounds. Like several victims before him, Coroner Wenz recorded that there was trauma to the head caused by an unknown object that punctured his forehead. The object had penetrated the brain, which caused hemorrhaging. It seemed Coeur d'Alene had an aggressive serial killer on the loose.

It was again the same strange square-shaped wound to the forehead, caused possibly by a handpick.

This victim had been dead between seven and ten days before being discovered. The deceased? A man named Christopher Kyriss.

Joe Johnson, the proprietor of the Franklin Hotel in Coeur d'Alene, had been Kyriss's friend for over seven years. He stated that at the time of his death, Kyriss had been renting a room at his hotel. He noted that when Kyriss was checking in, he appeared very nervous. He arrived alone and during the days Johnson saw him, and he was never seen with anyone else. When he ran into Kyriss the next morning after he checked in, he seemed upset, and when asked if he was going to go eat breakfast, Kyriss oddly replied, "Going to get a morning's morning, then go to breakfast."

Johnson had no inclination that that morning would be the very last time he ever saw his good friend Kyriss alive.

REWARD OF $500 FOR MURDERER

County Will Pay That for Conviction of Kyriss Slayer

Christopher Kyriss was found floating in the Coeur d'Alene River near downtown in 1908. His murder remains unsolved. *From the* Coeur d'Alene Evening Press, *June 1, 1908.*

Another pal, John Munch of Spokane, had been Kyriss's friend even longer, about nineteen years. He said he had last seen Kyriss on April 26. Although Kyriss had over $400 in the bank and would, at times, drink heavily and spend money freely, he was known to actually carry very little cash on his person.

His wife told reporters that the last time she saw her husband was on April 7. He told her he was going downtown to the meat market and that he would return soon. She noticed that he took with him two bank books, a six shooter and a change of shoes—strange items to take to the meat market.

When investigators questioned vendors at the meat market, it was discovered that Kyriss had ordered some meat and then, oddly, did not have the two dollars on him to pay for it. He told the butcher he was going to go to the bank to get the money he needed.

He never returned for his two-dollar meat purchase.

Why would he go to the meat market without any money? Was it just for show? Did he foretell his disappearance?

After the discovery of his body, both the Coeur d'Alene and Spokane police decided to work together on the case. They discovered that Kyriss had gone to Spokane on April 28 to pawn his gold watch. The pawn dealer told the police that Kyriss often pawned his watch for quick cash but always came back and retrieved it. It was a beautifully engraved watch with a heavy gold chain. They also learned that Kyriss had told a friend that he was going to travel to Ritzville to collect $800 that was owed to him. Who was the person who owed Kyriss such a large sum? And what was it for?

Coroner Wenz's autopsy reported that his forehead had certainly been penetrated by an object and that his lungs did not contain any water, so he was definitely killed prior to being tossed in the river. He also had a missing index finger on his left hand. Munch told police that the finger was missing a while ago, and that fact is what helped him identify the body of his friend. And what was the motive? Robbery? Murder for hire? Had he retrieved the $800 from the unknown person, only to have that person attack and kill him later? (Kyriss did not have the $800 cash on his person when his body was found.)

The police believed Kyriss had been tricked into getting drunk with someone and then lured to the area of Tubb's Hill, where he was assaulted, robbed and his body thrown into the lake.

Munch, very worried about what happened to Kyriss, went to the scene of the crime and found Kyriss's hat and coat placed neatly on a tree stump near where his body was found. He thought this was odd. Did Kyriss or his assailant neatly place his coat and hat on the stump? Why?

A $500 reward was offered by the county for information leading to the arrest of Kyriss's murder.

No one was ever arrested or convicted of the crime.

The horrible murder of Christopher Kyriss remains unsolved to this very day.

The summer of the next year brought several more bodies from the lake to the coroner's morgue.

One year later, the cold lake brought the grisly remains of another body to the shore near Lake Coeur d'Alene on the morning of May 24. The decomposed remains of J.T. Tennant, a resident of Coeur d'Alene, were found floating in the water near the mill of the Coeur d'Alene Lumber Company. The body was wrapped and taken to the morgue of the Coeur d'Alene Undertaking and examined by Coroner Wenz. The victim resembled Tennant, and several people were positive of the identity. One friend, George Otts, was certain it was Tennant.

He told police that Tennant had lived in Coeur d'Alene for about one and a half years but could not secure full-time employment. He completed odd jobs around town, including working for Judge Steele. Right before Tennant's disappearance, Steele had given Tennant a severe lecture about curbing his destructive heavy drinking habits. Tennant was living at a room in the Garland House on Fourth Street, and his landlady offered that he was past due on the rent and currently held no real job. She thought perhaps he had died by suicide.

Locals thought for sure it was the body of the missing J.T. Tannent, but they were wrong.

The body ended up being that of another doomed man named William Ingstrom, who had been missing since April 6 (curiously, just one day before Christenson and Collins mysteriously drowned and died).

Ingstrom was employed at the nearby Blackwell Lumber Mill. His wife last saw him the night before around 11:00 p.m. when he came home drunk. She remarked that he had an incredible (and unusual) one hundred dollars in cash on him. She tried to get him to go sleep the booze off somewhere else, like a nearby boardinghouse, but this only angered him. He was said to have paid their landlady the two-weeks-late rent earlier that day and then asked her for five dollars back. He assured her that he would return the borrowed five dollars as soon as the banks opened in the morning. Officers discovered that he had spent the day drinking in a saloon with two unidentified men and was last seen wearing a dark brown suit, the same one the body had been found clothed in. His friends believed Ingstrom had certainly met with foul play.

Where or from whom did he get the one hundred dollars from? Was he also gambling at the saloons and got lucky? Was the motive for murder to retrieve lost funds from the poker table that afternoon?

No more information can be found about Ingstrom, and no follow-up investigation by police seems to have occurred. His murder also remains unsolved to this day.

In early June, the river gave up its dead once again. An unidentified body was found floating in the river near St. Joe just six miles from Coeur d'Alene. The original location where the body was dumped was unknown. The body was discovered by a river pilot and taken to town by Coeur d'Alene Undertaking. No more information can be found about the identity of the floater and no follow up investigation seems to have occurred. Why?

On a crisp, clear morning at 9 a.m. on July 27th a body was found floating at the end of the Gunderson dock by a worker. The body was removed by Lemmer Undertaking to be examined later. The victim was wearing a dark coat, heavy flannel underwear and canvas shoes. He was clean shaven. In his pockets were a five dollar bill, a comb, gloves, a small knife and a five cent piece. His watch had stopped at 12:37 a.m. He was approximately five feet, six inches tall and a laborer. He had a scar on his left cheek and suffered a puncture wound to his right temple, like some of the other river victims. Deputy Sheriff Dyer was called to investigate the crime. He felt the man was another unfortunate woodsman.

Soon, another body was found. This unidentified man was only five feet tall, about 160 pounds and around thirty-five years of age. The only possessions on him at the time his body was discovered was a one dollar silver coin and some wet matches. Was he another victim of the river killer? No more information can be found about the identity of the floater, and no follow-up investigation seems to have occurred.

1908: JOE JURAS KILLS STEVE PASTORS OVER A CARD GAME

What started as a friendly game of cards and a few drinks ended as a horrible tragedy. Joe Juras, Steve Pastors, John Gryniski, Joe Matika and other employees of the Lewis Lumber Company (at 319 Sherman Street) got together for a night of fun at Jura's home in Coeur d'Alene. Juras was originally from Slavonia, Croatia.

After several hours of drinking and gambling, most of the men went home for the night. Juras and Pastors continued to drink and eventually ended up in an argument. The heated debate from an old feud continued until finally

Juras grabbed a butcher knife from the kitchen and stabbed Pastors several times in the back.

Juras admitted to the jury during his trial that he had stabbed Pastors while he was talking to his wife in their bedroom.

Witnesses told other versions of the senseless murder.

Witness 1: John Gryniski

Gryniski told the jury that Juras and his wife were in the bedroom when Pastors came in and started a conversation with the wife. The angry Juras went into the kitchen and grabbed a knife, went back to the bedroom and stabbed Pastors while he was leaning over the bed.

Witness 2: Joe Matika

Matika told the jury that he saw Juras and Pastors arguing and Juras then called Pastors into the kitchen, where the stabbing took place. Pastors yelled for Matika to come into the kitchen to get the knife away from Juras. Matika did as instructed and was able to wrangle the weapon away from Juras and put it in his pocket. He later turned the knife over to the police. After the victim was stabbed, he struggled and walked about ten feet, then fell to the floor and died an hour later.

Witness 3: Doctor Max Dorland

Dr. Dorland was in charge of examining the body of Pastors. He noted that the victim had suffered a stab wound on his left side, which penetrated his lung and severed a main artery. There existed a few other superficial wounds on his shoulder and back, but neither of those wounds was fatal.

THE DEFENSE ATTORNEYS FOR Juras, John Flynn and F.A. McCall, concluded that there was no blood found in the bedroom, but a large amount of blood had been found in the kitchen. Thus, the stabbing could not have taken place in the bedroom. They believed Pastors came into the kitchen, where the arguing continued, and that Pastors grabbed Juras by the throat and began choking him. Juras, in fear for his life, stabbed Pastors in self-defense.

After hearing all the evidence, the jury concluded that Juras was guilty of manslaughter.

Judge Chamberlain sentenced Juras to five years in the state penitentiary. Oddly, the judge put a $500 bail over Gryniski's head, which, of course, he could not pay. Deputy Sheriff Adams was put in charge of hauling both Juras and Gryniski off to the jail in Rathdrum. It is unclear why the judge ordered Gryniski to go to jail, as he tried to rescue Pastors and even gave the police the murder weapon.

Juras's wife, Elva, was pregnant at the time of the murder. Since she could not speak English, was uneducated, did not work and had no means of supporting herself and the coming baby, she was sent to the County Poor House. Eventually, she managed to apply for money to be transported back to Austria, where her family lived. The county decided to grant her the money, as it was cheaper to do that than to continue to care for Elva and her child.

1908: GAMBLING LEADS TO MURDER AND THEN SUICIDE

Mark McClammy was a Coeur d'Alene resident whose life took a tragic and horrific turn for the worse.

The story starts a year before the murderous/suicidal affair, when the couple was married in Eddy, New Mexico, in 1897. The abuse suffered by Etta during their marriage began on Thanksgiving Day in 1903 and continued to worsen as the years went by.

In 1907, Mr. McClammy purchased a small house from P.T. Nixon, located on the corner of Ninth and Wallace Streets in Coeur d'Alene for $2,750, in the hopes of moving his family in and starting over.

But the McClammys were having marital difficulties that Mrs. McClammy felt were beyond repair. This was coupled with her complete lack of desire to make the marriage work.

The couple had moved to Coeur d'Alene from Sandpoint in the hopes that a change could invigorate their love for one another, but it did not work. Mr. McClammy was a notorious gambler and was known to be abusive to his wife. Proprietor Doc Brown would testify that he was a regular at his Owl Saloon in Spokane. Mrs. McClammy had fallen in front of the Mott Block in Spokane the year before and sued the city for damages. She won the case, and soon, the couple was $7,000 richer. Mr. McClammy took half of the money and, returning to Sand Point, desired to open a gambling hall, but that line of work would only increase his drinking and gambling problems. Luckily, the deal fell through.

When he would become intoxicated, he would threaten to kill his wife. A restraining order was finally put into effect.

The terrified Mrs. McClammy promptly left her husband again and returned to the safety of Coeur d'Alene. She was tired of his drama and filed for a divorce after his final threat on New Year's Day in 1908. She was soon sitting in the lawyers' offices of Black, Wernette and E.N. LaVeine. Mr. McClammy did not take to the divorce kindly and threatened to kill her if she followed through with the suit. He also threatened to kill her lawyers.

Running for her life again, on January 19, she packed her things and decided to move herself, her five-year-old daughter, Eva, and eight-year-old son, Harold, to a room on the third floor in the Pedicord Hotel in Spokane, hoping to hide there until the divorce was finalized. Without looking back, they boarded the last train from Coeur d'Alene to Spokane, hoping to finally get some much-needed peace form the troublesome situation.

On January 20, in retaliation for filing for divorce, Mr. McClammy quickly marched over to Sheriff McGovern's office and demanded Etta be arrested on the grounds that she had embezzled $750 and abducted their children.

For some reason, Judge Steele signed off on the ridiculous charges, and Etta was found by the police and arrested at the Pedicord Hotel. She was later dismissed of the charges.

Pedicord Hotel.

The tension continued between the couple. Although Etta tried to surround herself with her friends for safety, her plan did not work.

On February 16, as soon as Mr. McClammy found out his wife's whereabouts, he, too, rented a room at the Pedicord Hotel. He tried to reconcile with his wife daily, which she desperately wanted no part of. More threats from him followed.

Perhaps Etta should have taken his rants about killing her more seriously.

On the afternoon of February 23, his horrific threats became a reality. After talking things over for more than an hour in the hallway of the hotel, McClammy began to finally realize he was never going to be able to persuade his wife to return to him. In a huff, he stormed off down the hall.

Etta quickly closed the door, hoping that was the end of it.

But it wasn't.

The very angry Mark McClammy, wielding a .38-caliber pistol, marched back to her room, the gun hidden in his waistcoat. He demanded she open the door once again for him.

When she answered the door, he asked her again if she would return to him, and she simply replied, "No, I will not."

This was the last time Etta would argue with her husband.

Their frightened young son stood silently nearby, witnessing the horrible arguing between his parents.

Frustrated, Mark commented to Etta, "Well, then this ends everything between us," and quickly drew his concealed gun.

Etta had no time to retreat or close the door.

Without hesitation, he calmly shot his wife four times.

The hotel's maid, Lucy Smith, stood nearby, frozen in fear, and then immediately ran down the stairs, screaming at the top of her lungs for help. The insane Mr. Clammy then turned the gun on himself, pointing the weapon precisely at his right temple, and pulled the trigger, killing himself instantly.

The surprised hotel help soon arrived at the bloody scene. They carefully assisted Mrs. McClammy to her bed and then quickly called for a doctor and the police.

The police arrived and immediately called for the undertaker to come to the Pedicord Hotel; it was obvious Mr. McClammy was dead. His body was taken to the Buchanan Morgue in Spokane.

The doctor and nurse arrived and ran to Etta's bedside, hoping to give her some relief or somehow save her.

They concluded that Etta had suffered from three of the four gunshots; one bullet hit her liver, a second bullet pierced below her heart and a third shattered her wrist. The doctor and nurse shook their heads in unison. Sadly, she would not survive the attack.

The two horrified small children stood near their dying mother, forever traumatized by the scenario.

Etta soon fell into a coma. The physician made her comfortable with an injection of morphine. For the next hour, Etta moved in and out of consciousness.

At one point, she was clear enough to tell her nurse, "Please don't let me die yet. I want to see a minister. Keep me alive as long as you can."

The good Reverend C. William Giboney (or Gibboney) of the nearby Presbyterian church rushed to her bedside and offered his help. Etta begged him to baptize her. As soon as the reverend completed his impromptu baptism, she fell back into a coma.

Little Eva came to her mother's bedside and sat silently. She held a ripe orange in the hopes of giving the produce to her mom. Etta seemed to waken for just a moment and smiled at her daughter. It was the last time the two would interact.

Then a nurse came to her bed side to check on her bandages. Etta reached for the woman's hand and quietly told the lady, "I know the end is near, and under no circumstances is my body to be buried next to that of my husband." The nurse and reverend nodded and reassured the dying woman they would carry out her final request.

Etta died at 4:48 p.m. at the Pedicord Hotel from her gunshot wounds on February 24.

Soon, the bodies of both Mr. and Mrs. McClammy lay together in the morgue at Buchanan's.

The brother of Mr. McClammy, known only as R.P., arrived from Montana to take the children. Other references say the children went to live with the Boone family in California.

Both of the bodies are buried in Spokane, but as promised, the two lie apart in eternal peace.

Etta was only thirty-eight years old at the time of her murder. It is a very sad and unfortunate outcome, as the restraining order to protect her life was in place but obviously not enforced by local authorities. After suffering years of abuse, she simply wanted to move on from her married life and create a safe and loving environment for her and her two small children. Yet her life was cut short in the most horrible manner by the hands of a man she (at one time) loved and trusted enough to marry.

HUSBAND DEAD
WIFE IS DYING

Mark McClammy Attempts Murder and Commits Suicide.

Mark McClammy shot his wife and then killed himself in 1908 in front of his children. *From the* Spokane Press, *February 24, 1908.*

1909: Man Kills Another over a Shaving Razor

A cold-blooded killer fled to Coeur d'Alene after savagely murdering a man over a shaving razor. Arthur B.P. Smith (also known as A.K. Kreek) of Coeur d'Alene shot and killed Eth Hoffman in the summer of 1909. The only witness was a young girl who saw the crime through the window of her family's kitchen. Smith was later captured while riding aboard the steamer *Milwaukie* on the Coeur d'Alene River.

The strange scenario began when Smith stole a shaving razor from Hoffman. He quickly began walking down the road, excited that he had gotten away with stealing it. Much to his dismay, Hoffman was hot on his trail, carrying a big club with which he was going to teach Smith a very tough lesson in committing robbery.

As soon as Hoffman caught up with the villain, he began hitting Smith over the head and shoulders with the wooden club. After a few blows, Smith realized that Hoffman meant business, so he pulled his hidden gun from his vest and fired a few shots at him. The first shot did not stop the angry Hoffman, so Smith fired his revolver once more.

After Smith was apprehended, he told the police, "I did not think I actually killed the man. I tied a hanky around his neck to stop the flow of blood. Then I ran north, and after I had hid my pack in the bushes, I ran west and came to Spokane through Minnehaha Park."

Apparently, he then went toward East Sprague Avenue and continued on to the OR&N Depot to take a freight train out of town. But when he discovered there were no trains leaving soon, he changed course and found a hotel to hide in for the night. He registered under the false name of James Dean.

The next morning, Smith walked along the tracks until he found his way to Blackwell's Lumber Camp on Coeur d'Alene Lake.

Smith realized he needed money to escape, so he worked a few days at the mill until Friday came along. With a few bucks in his pocket, he made his way to Mica Bay then took a boat headed for Coeur d'Alene. He was hoping to get to Dudley, find his uncle and hopefully secure a job working in the Coeur d'Alene mines. He told anyone who would listen that he killed Hoffman in self-defense and said he was sure he would not get into any trouble over the matter.

But he didn't elude the police for long.

Once captured, he tried to tell prosecuting attorney Fred Pugh that the slight scratches on his arms and face were caused by the severe and murderous clubbing he had received from Hoffman. When the jurors' eyes rolled at this comment, Smith recanted his story and admitted the scratches were from the bushes where he hid his pack, not from Hoffman. He did confess to putting the stolen razor in his victim's pocket before he ran away from the body.

Pugh told the *Coeur d'Alene Evening Press* on July 19:

> *We can make a case of at least manslaughter against Smith. The outcome of it may be more serious than that for him. There is every indication that the crime was deliberate. Smith had two revolvers, just alike. He threw one of them into the river at D Street when he arrived in the city and the other he sent to the bottom of the Coeur d'Alene River from the steamer* Milwaukiee. *He is known to have tried to pose as a bad man, exhibiting his guns and telling of exploits which never were enacted except in his own mind.*

Smith was taken to the county jail to await his trial. While he was in custody, Smith was arrogant and jovial.

After an intense interrogation, he was loaded into a police car along with Deputy Sheriffs M.F. Ryan and Thomas Heddle and the attorney Pugh. With Smith's instructions, they drove back to the scene of the crime, where Hoffman's bloody body was found. They also made him drive to where he had hidden his backpack.

When confronted with his grave situation and sure guilt, Smith made a very bizarre announcement: "You fellows have got me, and you can just dip in and take your mustard!"

Witness 1

The impressionable thirteen-year-old Maggie Becker told her version of the murder:

> *I was looking out the window, and I saw Smith coming along the road. I was looking at him through a field glass. He was a smooth-faced man. He had on dark clothes and a black hat. He was carrying a pack on his back. When he was in front of our house, I saw Eth come running along the road. He caught up with Smith, and I saw Smith turn around and put down his pack. Eth had a club in his hands, and he hit Smith twice on the back with it. Smith had his face turned toward our house and was just putting his pack on the ground when Eth hit him. When Smith put his*

pack on the ground and rose up, he took a pistol out of his pocket and shot three times. I think he shot three times before Eth fell. I was so scared that I ran away from the window and did not look out again. I told Papa about it when he got home.

Witness 2

Hoffman's uncle J.W. Parker also testified. He stated:

I was driving south on my way to Roberts' Store. I passed a man who was walking north. He had a pack on his back and walking fast. A couple of minutes later, Eth Hoffman came along the road. He was running, and when I asked him if he was in a hurry, he said, "Yes. I am going to catch that feller." I thought no more about it until I heard that Eth had been shot. Eth did not have a club on him when I met him.

Witness 3

John Fuher of Fuher's Mill told the police:

I discharged Smith Saturday morning. I did not know the man by that name, but the man who was working for me fits that description. He told me his name was A.K. Kreek. He went to work for me that July 5th, and last Friday, he told me he wanted to quit. Saturday morning, I told him I would like to have him stay, but he said his arm was too sore to work. When he turned his back to me, I saw the handle of the revolver sticking out of his pocket. I did not like that, and I told him I would pay him off. I started to write a check, but being suspicious of the man, I paid him cash. He left about 9 o'clock, and soon after, that Hoffman said he missed his razor. He started out after the Smith, and that was the last I saw of him alive.

The coroner reported that Hoffman suffered from three shots: one in the neck, two inches below his ear; another in his forehead; and a third in his neck (probably while he was already down). There were two handkerchiefs tied around his neck, one red and one white. His hat had been pulled down over his eyes.

After the trial, the jury came back with the verdict that Hoffman had died from gunshot wounds inflicted by Arthur B.P. Smith.

One of the strangest parts of the story is that for some reason, Smith had been released (or escaped) from custody.

A report came into the sheriff's office at 9:00 p.m. on July 12 that said a man appearing like Smith was seen near Minnehaha Park. Deputy Sheriffs Tom Heddle, John Mills and S.D. Doak quickly made their way to Minnehaha Park in the hopes of securing their killer.

But the lucky Smith was nowhere to be found. Sheriff Pugh and Sweet worked all day and night trying to locate Smith. For days, they searched all over Coeur d'Alene in the hopes that Smith would return to meet friends or family there.

No further information can be found about Smith or his whereabouts. He does not show up in the records of the Idaho State Penitentiary under his real or assumed names.

So, Smith got away with murder, and Hoffman lost his life over a shaving razor.

1914: Two Men Dead over Two Suitcases

Considered one of the most cold-blooded murders in all of Kootenai County's history is the killing of George "Shorty" Archer. His murder seemed senseless to local citizens and his fellow employees at the Grant Lumber Company. Another man (known only as Bob), innocent of any known crimes, was also murdered in cold blood.

It all started during the summer of 1914 near O'Gara's Landing near the St. Joe River just outside of Coeur d'Alene. The area had been experiencing a lot of petty crime during that period, so everyone was on guard.

Around 2:00 p.m., two men, George Archer and Grant Redfield, were returning to Grant's Camp after a long morning of work. Upon entering their quarters, they noticed that their suitcases had been stolen. Angered, Archer grabbed his .22-caliber gun, and the men set out on foot in search of the thief.

They did not have to walk far. They soon came upon a homeless man walking the dirt road with a suitcase in his hand. Archer immediately noticed that it was his case and approached the man, waving his gun around.

"Where is the other suitcase?" Archer yelled to the stranger.

The stranger confessed and said, "It is over there in the gulch. Just stay here. I will go get it."

Archer felt confident he had scared the man into submission, so he sat down on a log and waited for the man to return with his friend's suitcase. He never lowered his gun from the man's direction.

But after a few seconds, the stranger emerged from the ravine, turned toward Archer and fired a gun at him. Then he fired a second shot.

Archer died immediately, as the first fatal bullet struck him in his right breast, and the second bullet entered just inches below the first. Witnesses nearby heard both shots being fired.

Word got out quickly that Archer had been killed by an unknown assailant. Sheriff Bailey, Deputy Sawyer and attorney N.D. Wernette were quick to arrive on the scene by boat. They immediately formed a posse and began searching for the killer. They rode through Fred Hess's ranch and headed through the bushes in hot pursuit. They came across two armed men hiding in the thicket.

One of the men raised his gun at the lawmen, and Sawyer quickly shot at the man. The bullet pierced through a main artery and killed the man almost instantly. Sawyer quickly asked the dying man if he had been the one who killed Archer. The bleeding man simply said, "No, no, I did not kill any man."

Sheriff Bailey promptly handcuffed him and took the gun away from the other stranger. His captive fit the description given to them from witnesses at Grant's Camp. He asked the man what his friend's name was, and he said that he only knew the man as Bob. He claimed his own name was S.S. Burke.

Bailey and Sawyer dragged both men, one dead and one handcuffed, back to Coeur d'Alene. Burke went to jail, and Bob went to the morgue.

In the jail, Burke told his attorney, Dwight Leeper from Coeur d'Alene, that he was lured into the ravine by Archer, who threatened to kill him if he did not return the other suitcase. He stated that he shot Archer in self-defense.

But Burke's story quickly changed. Later, he told the judge that Archer was actually killed by his twin brother, Stanley Austin, who had just rolled in from La Grande, Oregon. The judge did not buy his story. Neither did the jury. After just three hours of deliberation, the jury came back with the verdict of guilty for second-degree murder, which sentenced Burke to a minimum of twenty years to life in prison.

S.S. Burke was a mere nineteen years old at the time he committed Archer's murder.

Burke was taken to Boise State Penitentiary on October 4, 1914, and he was listed as convict no. 2206. His final sentence was between ten and twenty years in prison.

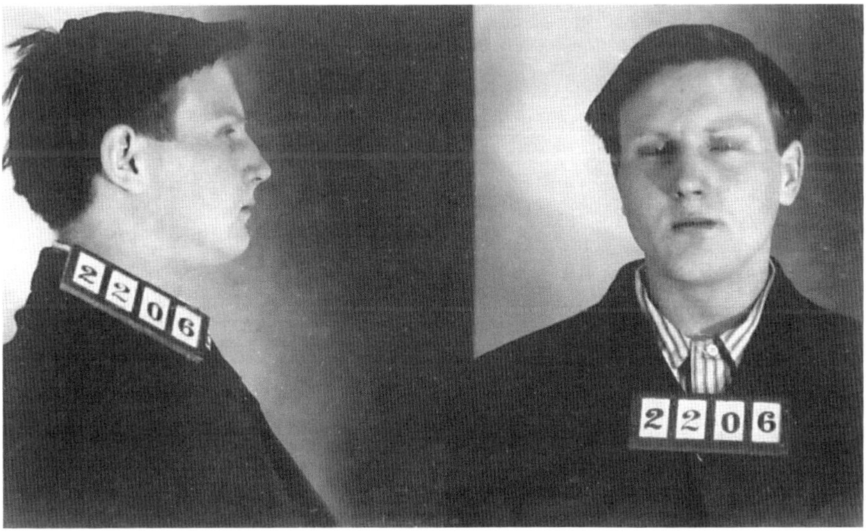

Top: In 1914, S.S. Burke killed George Archer over a stolen suitcase. He later claimed his twin brother did the crime. *Courtesy of the Idaho State Penitentiary and Ancestry.*

Bottom: A mug shot of S.S. Burke's brother, Stanley Austin. The two looked nothing alike, so Burke's ridiculous claim that his brother shot Archer was quickly dismissed. *Courtesy of the Idaho State Penitentiary and Ancestry.*

Born in 1895, Burke came from a hard past. Both his parents died when he was young, and he took to living on the streets at the early age of ten. It is unclear if he actually had a twin brother, although a Stanley Austin Burke was previously booked in the Montana State Penitentiary as convict no. 3661.

If you examine the two photographs included in this section, the brothers look nothing alike.

1914: Death over Dinner

An untimely death over dinner seems like an unusual way to die, but it actually happened on December 1, 1914, in a small cabin that a man named H.C. Jones owned in the woods along the Milwaukie Railroad tracks, just outside of Coeur d'Alene.

What started out as a fun get-together between two brothers and a longtime friend ended in a bloody tragedy and family heartache.

The Plunkett brothers, known as Charles E. and H.H., lived and worked in Spokane and frequented the home of their friend H.C. Jones in Coeur d'Alene. During this particular trip, the brothers were scheduled to work at the nearby Anderson farm. They fatally decided to bring two quarts of whiskey along for the trip. Around 11:00 p.m., the three men settled in at the small cabin for a quiet night of gambling, drinking and cooking together.

But after a few too many drinks, Jones became quarrelsome. In an effort to try to keep the peace and sober everyone up, Charles decided to cook supper for the men. Unfortunately, Charles was so drunk, he stumbled around the cook stove and dropped the dinner on the floor. This infuriated Jones to no end.

H.H. was not feeling very well. He had only one drink all day and became sleepy, so he snuck out of the room and went to bed around 7:00 p.m.

But his slumber was cut short by the sounds of the two men arguing loudly in the kitchen. Jones was still angry about the spoiled food.

H.H. heard Jones scream that he wanted to kill him.

Charles yelled back at Jones, "Shoot me or don't shoot me!"

Jones in turn yelled, "This is the way I will fix you!" He then grabbed his gun and brought it down on the man's head, knocking him to the floor, unconscious. H.H. tried to remain calm in the tiny room nearby. He peered out into the kitchen area and saw his brother Charles lying on the floor, his head bleeding.

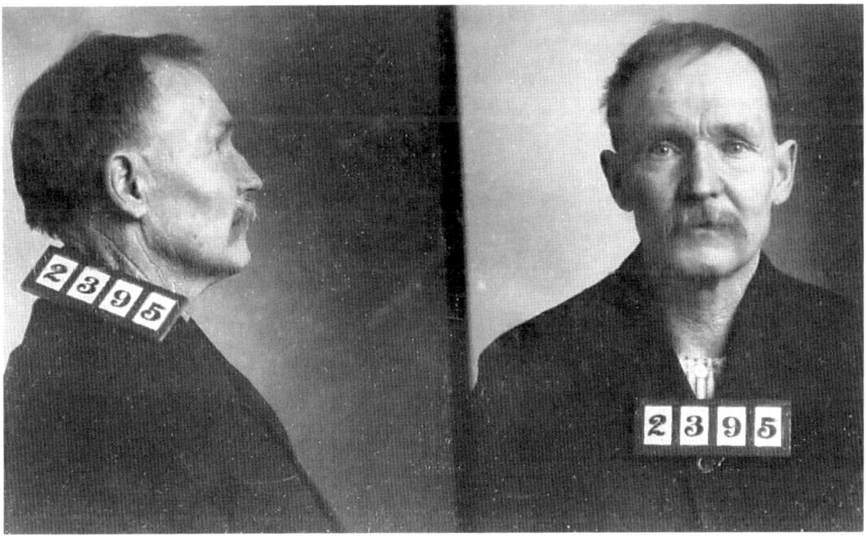

A mug shot of H.C. Jones, who violently killed one of his friends, Charles Plunkett, in 1914 over a burned supper. *Courtesy of the Idaho State Penitentiary and Ancestry.*

What he witnessed next was horrifying.

Jones peered through his blood-shot eyes and slowly pointed his gun directly at the head of the defenseless Charles.

Boom! He pulled the trigger. The sound of the gunshot rang through the tiny cabin.

As he watched his brother be killed in cold blood by Jones, H.H. froze in fear. Jones then looked back at H.H. with hate in his eyes.

Jones casually and slowly walked over and said, "Pick him up and put him on the bed."

H.H. tried in vain to lift his brother's heavy body, but he was too weak and scared.

"Try again," demanded Jones nudging him with the revolver, "or I will shoot your head off, too!"

With a sudden found strength, H.H. was able to lift his dead brother's corpse enough to get it to the bed. Just then, Jones misstepped, staggered and fell to the ground.

H.H. saw this as the only opportunity he would have to save his own life from Jones's drunken tirade. He quickly ran from the cabin and fled into the woods as fast as he could run.

Luckily, Jones did not follow him.

Outside, H.H. flagged down an oncoming Milwaukie passenger train and begged for help.

The engineer contacted the local police.

Sheriff Sawyer and Dr. O.D. Platt (or Clapp) returned to the crime scene to arrest Jones and investigate the murder. When they arrived, Jones was passed out in a chair, sleeping, and Charles's blood-soaked body was lying on the bed, right where H.H. had left it.

Sawyer quickly handcuffed and arrested the unconscious Jones. The victim's body and Jones were both transported back to Coeur d'Alene—Jones straight to jail and Charles to the morgue.

As the doctor examined the victim, he recorded that the bullet had passed through the man's right breast and lodged in his right shoulder. The man also suffered from a deep wound to the top of his head, where Jones had bludgeoned him with the butt of his revolver. Surprisingly, the skull was not fractured. He also noted that C.E. Plunkett's lungs had filled with blood and that the cause of death was internal bleeding caused by the gunshot wound.

Charles E. Plunkett was born in Indiana in 1880 and was only thirty-four years old when he was killed.

Jones was born in North Carolina in 1857 and worked as a railroad engineer for most of his life. Jones had a different version of the night of the murder. He claimed that (although he was so drunk, he did not remember most of the evening) he became angry at Charles because he left his buck knife on the stove. The two began to argue. Charles, a much bigger man, attacked Jones during the fight. The two struggled. Jones then grabbed his rifle from under the bed, and somehow, during the struggle, the gun was discharged, killing Charles instantly.

There are several holes in his story:

- The cabin was very small, and the other Plunkett brother was sleeping on the bed. He would have been woken by Jones's attempt to grab the rifle from under the bed.
- H.H. actually witnessed Jones shooting his brother at point-blank range. H.H. was not under the influence of alcohol during the time of the murder.
- H.H. did not witness any struggle other than when Jones hit his brother over his head prior to shooting him.

The county attorney filed for Jones to be tried for murder in the second degree when he was fifty-nine years old. Unluckily for him, the fourteen months he served in the Coeur d'Alene jail did not go toward his sentence at the state penitentiary. The law at the time was written that the prisoner's sentenced time actually started at the time of their entry to the state prison. Time spent in any other prison did not count toward their sentence. Jones had a $3,500 bail over his head, which he had no way of securing. Later in 1915, Jones's attorney, F.C. Smith, filed a 299-page appeal requesting a new trial. The reasons for the new trial did not impress the judge. The jury debated for about five hours but eventually found Jones indeed guilty of murder in the second degree. Judge Dunn ordered Deputy Sheriff Toohey to transport Jones from Spokane to Boise.

He was logged as inmate no. 2395 in the Boise State Penitentiary for a sentence that would run between two and ten years.

For unknown reasons, in 1917, a group of citizens started a petition for Jones's release from prison, requesting a pardon from the state board.

2
SILVER VALLEY MURDERS

I say a murder is abstract. You pull the trigger, and after that,
you do not understand anything that happens.
—Jean-Paul Sartre

The many expansive fortunes to be made in northern Idaho from the valuable silver and gold extracted from the mountains began to flow in the mid-1800s. Captain Elias Davidson Pierce and his friend first discovered gold in the north fork of the Clearwater River on February 20, 1860. This was the start of a small stampede. (And the search for silver and gold in the Silver Valley continues to this day.)

Years later, in November 1889, prospector Jack Breen also found gold near Coeur d'Alene. Unfortunately for Breen, he was broke and had no money to actually work his newfound discovery. The eager Breen soon got locals N.R. Palmeter and Jack Osier to take a chance on the claim and invest some money into working it. To seal their decision, the men went to a nearby saloon and proceeded to celebrate their soon-to-be-made fortune by drinking whiskey together. When the word got out that Breen had discovered gold, opportunity-seeking men gathered around Breen and his pals and began buying them drinks, hoping he would spill the location of the discovery. But Breen was smarter than they thought and would only say that it was "somewhere near Hayden Lake." But the men continued to prod and threaten Breen for information.

The event of a public hanging was a big deal and drew a fantastic crowd. Often, there were invitations sent out to a select few, and being invited was considered a fantastic privilege. *Courtesy of the Library of Congress, no. 2012646359.*

Soon, the local Marshall got wind that the men were trying to take advantage of the intoxicated Breen, so he put him in jail to protect him from the thugs and let him sober up a bit in the safety of a cell.

Tragically, the very next morning the jail mysteriously caught fire, and Breen died. Was it murder or an accident? Did one of the men from the bar seek revenge for Breen keeping the location of the gold a secret?

To this day, the exact location of Breen's gold discovery is unknown, and his secret went to his grave with him.

Murder was somewhat commonplace during the 1800s. And back in the old days, the penalty for killing someone was "death by hanging" and occurred within months—not through decades of trials and appeals as it does today.

The event of a public hanging was a big deal and drew a fantastic crowd. Often, there were invitations sent out to a select few, and being invited was considered a fantastic privilege.

An example of a cold-blooded murder that occurred over a very trivial thing was a killing that happened one dark night in October 1911. A hard-looking man with a face blackened by soot came barging into a saloon in Wallace. He pointed his gun at the patrons and yelled, "Hands up!"

Everyone in the room quickly threw their hands into the air as ordered—except one man. An old prospector named Owen Perry from Kellogg apparently moved too slowly for the robber. Perhaps the man was feeble. Perhaps he had an injury in his shoulders. Or perhaps he did just move too slowly.

Regardless, it cost him his life. The robber pointed his gun at Perry and shot him dead on the spot in front of many witnesses.

Perry was a well-respected old-timer who worked his claim up on Pine Creek, a few miles from Kellogg, Idaho.

As of 1912, it was recorded that his unknown assailant was still at large, and the senseless murder was never solved.

There are many old, recorded and unsolved murders that took place in the Silver Valley and Kootenai County. Unfortunately, it seems people either felt the bugger deserved to die or, since no one put up a fuss about arresting the perpetrator, the killing earned mothing more than a sentence (or two) in the local paper.

One such strange murder was that of a miner from Finland named John Macki. He came to the United States with his father in 1901. He went to school for three days. From 1907 onward, Macki was an active member in the Western Federation of Miners in Minnesota, giving interviews in order to voice the opinions of the men. They felt the mines should belong to the men, not companies or mine owners. Many were socialists who believed the miners should only work an eight-hour day (not the typical fourteen hours, working from 6:00.a.m to 8:00 p.m. for a measly three dollars). They also felt it was unfair that they had to buy their own dynamite for the job, which could drop their wage lower—to just two dollars a day. Unfair, indeed.

Not much more information can be found out about Macki from 1907 onward, until he was brutally murdered in 1921.

What is known?

Macki was last seen alive the day before his murder. His body was found on October 17, 1921, somewhere near Lookout Pass (a few miles past Mullen, Idaho) in an area known as the O'Brien Gulch. The thirty-eight-year-old man was executed at point-blank range by several bullets to the back of his head. Not much more information is given about the event; though oddly, there are a few photographs in the Bernard-Stockbridge

Collection (in the museum in Wallace, Idaho) that offer images of the recreation of the incident.

His death certificate, no. 36186 issued by the State of Idaho, simply states his cause of death "gunshot wounds from person unknown." Why was he killed? Who killed him? Neither his killer nor their motive was ever discovered.

The photographed reenactment is curious. Why was his murder important enough to warrant a reenactment that was professionally photographed but not worthy of an ongoing investigation?

Many of the murders carried in the Silver Valley went unsolved—some didn't even warrant a proper investigation.

1863: THE HORRIFIC MAGRUDER CLAN MURDERS

Nothing could be more horrendous than the gruesome, pathetic and brutal killing of an innocent, hardworking man named Lloyd Magruder Jr. (1825–1863).

He came to his grisly end one dark night in the summer of 1863 at the hands of a group of trusted men who were traveling with him and his train of mules, supplies and a large amount of gold dust.

The murder was considered one of north Idaho's "most wicked" crimes and is one that lingered in the locals' minds long after they finished reading about it. The incident eventually led to the first legal hangings in Idaho Territory. The Magruder clan's brutal multiple murders and how they were eventually supernaturally solved by Magruder's best friend are definitely the makings of a movie.

The tale begins in the 1860s, when Magruder began packing and selling mining supplies over the mountains. He was a well-respected, prominent citizen and one of the state's oldest pioneers, as he came to work in Idaho around 1862. He was one of the very first trail makers into the untamed Canyon Creek area. He was also one of the leaders in the discovery of the profitable John Day Mine.

Magruder also owned a profitable grocery store, and they say it was at his very own store that Magruder met the murderous men who later traveled with him and sealed his tragic fate.

In 1863, Magruder moved his work on from Lewiston, Idaho, to the Bannock Mines in Montana with fifty head of mules, eight horses and a good load of supplies. But when he got there, the Bannock mines were

A very rare photograph of Lloyd Magruder, who was brutally murdered (along with his crew) while running his mule team and supplies through the mountains. *Courtesy of Liz O'Hara, the great-great-granddaughter of Lloyd Magruder.*

almost empty, as most men had moved on to a new discovery located at Grasshopper Creek. Another gold rush was discovered at Virginia City, so many men also traveled there to seek their fortunes.

But the entrepreneurial part of Magruder was not discouraged. He set up a makeshift shop anyway and sold his wares, traded some mules and sold supplies, which earned him a very hefty chunk of change. Stories vary, but it is said he managed to sell about $15,000 worth of goods and mules and was then the proud owner of approximately ninety-four pounds of gold dust. (Gold dust was the only form of legal tender back then, as greenbacks were discounted and were frowned upon when used. This amount of gold dust would be worth almost $2 million today.)

Unfortunately, earning that kind of money in front of his crew was not very smart.

The men packed up and left Bannock to make their way back to Lewiston. It was a long, lonesome and winding three hundred miles home on the back of a horse or in a wagon.

Three shifty men soon caught wind of Magruder's money and began to devise a plot to rob him. These three men were David Renton, George Christopher Lower (or Lowery) and James Romaine. They took another worker named Page aside and whispered their plan to rob and kill Magruder. But Page was no killer and wanted no part of their plan.

On October 3, the men set out to head back to Lewiston. On this particular trip, Magruder had no reason not to trust the group of men who accompanied him (their names vary): William Phillips, Charles Allen, Daniel "Doc" Howard, George Christopher Lowery, David Renton, James Romaine, William Page and two brothers named Horace and Robert Chalmers. Magruder hired the group to help handle and care for the mule train and for personal protection during the long three-hundred-mile journey. The men all seemed to get along and soon became friends. Some of the men offered much-needed services for the trip; Lowery was a trained blacksmith, "Doc" had good knowledge of medicine and Page was a trapper and guide and knew his way through the mountains.

A mule team (that was twice as long as this one from 1890) was used by Magruder. The assailants killed all but a few of Magruder's mules and several of his horses—after they bludgeoned the crew to death. *Courtesy of the Library of Congress, no. 2013647267.*

Yet it is still curious that Magruder felt safe enough to carry such a valuable amount of gold dust with him, even with what he thought was protection.

Five days into the trip, on the evening of October 8, the men decided to stop for the night and set up camp as usual. The group was tired, dusty, thirsty and hungry. But before retiring, a lot of work had to be done: a cook fire was made, makeshift tents were put together, a rope corral was built for the horses and mules, water had to be lugged from the creek for the animals, et cetera.

After all chores were done, Magruder and Lowery were scheduled to be on duty for the first watch. The rest of the men were bone tired and went to bed. After some relaxation by the fire, Magruder and Lowery heard the mules stomping around, so they decided to go check on them and also wanted to make sure they had water for the night. The men moved away from the warmth of the fire and into the cool darkness of the woods.

Magruder noticed that as he and Lowery walked toward the mules, Lowery had oddly clutched a nearby axe to take with them. Magruder paused for a minute and wondered why on earth Lowery would need an axe. When asked about it, Lowery claimed he was going to build a better fence to make sure the mules stayed put for the night. Magruder thought this was very strange and would be a lot of unnecessary work. If Magruder would have followed his intuition right then, he might have somehow survived the night.

Instead, the two men slowly walked together over to where the mules were being kept.

That was the last time Magruder would take a breath or look into the starry night.

Lowery quickly brought the axe down onto Magruder's skull, crushing it and killing him instantly.

Around midnight, back at the camp, Page heard Renton and Lowery talking outside. As he peered out, he did not see Magruder anywhere. Lowery looked like he had blood on his coat, and he was immediately suspicious. He saw the two men both carrying axes and quietly moving into the nearby tent. Much to Page's horror, moans and loud cries could be heard coming from the two brothers, Horace and Robert Chalmers, inside that tent.

Blood spatter spotted the canvas tent as they were hacked to pieces inside.

Then there was only silence—but not for long

The bloodied Renton quickly grabbed his gun and shot the stunned and terrified Charles Allen (who stood nearby in utter shock), killing him instantly. William Phillips stood frozen in fear, scared for his life, as he had just witnessed the men killing the others in cold blood.

Without hesitation, Romaine moved toward Phillips with the axe yelling, "You fool! I told you at Virginia City not to come. You had no business to come. I wish Jim Rhodes had come instead, for I have wanted to kill him for a long time!" Then he proceeded to quickly kill Phillips with the axe.

William Page stood completely paralyzed, knowing he would be the next victim in the bloody massacre.

As the men looked into each other's eyes, a silent meeting of the minds took place.

Surprisingly, the killers calmly told the terrified Page to go look after the mules.

Page was apparently spared his life only because he knew the routes like the back of his hand and could help them get back to town without getting lost.

Next, the murderers had to devise a plan to dispose of the evidence and the bodies. They sat by the fire together and came up with a solution. They decided to roll the bodies up in tent canvases and roll them down the nearby hill into a ravine. Back by the mules, Magruder's bloody body was still right where Lowery had left it. It was soon rolled up into a piece of canvas and tossed into the ravine, along with the other bodies. The rest of the travel bags, mountain gear and any evidence were thrown in the fire to burn. After the evidence was burned, they gathered up the remaining iron, put it in a bag and buried it under a big log nearby.

For some unknown reason (possibly because it would be highly suspicious if the men were seen traveling with Magruder's large team of mules without him), the killers decided to make the night even more horrific.

Instead of just setting the mules free, they shot almost all eighty mules, keeping only a few of the best ones, along with the eight horses.

Next, they took off their boots and put on moccasins, premeditating that if they wore the moccasins, whoever stumbled across the crime scene would think that the murders were done by Natives, not white men.

They then divvied up Magruder's gold, mounted their horses and headed back toward Lewiston as if nothing had happened. The terrified Page was leading the way back to civilization. Can you imagine what was going through the poor man's head as he traveled along the trails with these cold-blooded, greedy and ruthless killers? His terror and anxiety got greater day by day and mile by mile as they got closer to town. What if he led them close enough to town that they would not need his skill anymore? Would they just kill him, too, and leave him on the side of the trail?

There are no records of whether Page received any of the gold dust. One would assume they gave him some of the money in order to keep his mouth shut about what had happened.

Along the way, the men found a local rancher to take care of the extra horses, remaining mules and riding tack for them until spring, paying the rancher with Magruder's hard-earned money.

They finally made it back to Lewiston, and all of them were alive—even Page.

How the killers slept that night at the Hotel de France in Lewiston is a mystery. But the next morning, on October 19, they loaded their belongings up in a stagecoach and were soon headed toward Walla Walla, Washington.

But they did not plan on one strange thing that would eventually bring them to justice.

This is where the supernatural part comes into play.

The same night the killers murdered Lloyd Magruder, Magruder's best friend, Hilary "Hill" Beachy (1822–1875), had a gut-wrenching premonition in the form of a nightmare. In his dream, he had the sickening image of his friend Lloyd with his face hacked apart and his neck bloody—he had been killed by a man with an axe.

That night, when Beachy woke in a start, sweaty and shaken, he somehow knew his friend was dead. He didn't know how he knew it, but he did. Did his best friend really come to him in a dream to let him know of his terrible demise? Was it possible? Throughout the day, Beachy could not shrug off the dream no matter how hard he tried. He began asking around if anyone had seen Magruder lately. No one had.

Then when another packer came riding into Lewiston, a man who had left after Magruder, Beachy knew in his heart that Magruder had met trouble, as his friend should have arrived back into town days before this guy did.

Interestingly (and here is where an interesting coincidence comes into play), when the murderers inquired about four stage tickets for a coach that headed from Lewiston to Walla Walla, they did so at Beachy's own stagecoach line. And Beachy had another stroke of odd luck; he actually remembered and recognized one of the men's faces—from his dream.

But Beachy remained cool and calm behind his desk. He did not want to tip the men off and scare them away before he could hopefully secure more information about them and notify the sheriff. He quietly told the men that the office was currently closed but that he would take their names down on the waybill to secure seats for the morning's trip. They gave him the fake names of John and Joseph Smith and Tom and Jim Jones. Beachy became even more suspicious, as he could tell they were obviously lying.

As the men were checking into their rooms at the Hotel de France in town and getting ready to sleep off the long trip, Beachy decided he had to snoop around to find out more about these strangers. He went to his friend Judge John G. Berry's house to see if he could help him out.

Beachy and Berry soon discovered from locals that the suspects had boarded their horses at a nearby ranch, so they quickly mounted their horses and set out. Upon their arrival at the ranch, Beachy began looking over the horses that the men had left there, and he suddenly recognized Magruder's personal saddle was perched on a bale in the barn. His heart sank. He was pretty sure Magruder did not sell his favorite saddle to one of these rough-looking men. Why in the world would he need to sell his favorite saddle when Magruder had plenty of money? It did not make any sense. Beachy knew that Magruder had met with foul play.

Beachy was more certain than ever that the men had killed his friend and immediately began begging the judge to put out an arrest warrant for these four killers.

What was Beachy thinking? All of this speculation on a dream, a hunch and an abandoned saddle? It seemed ridiculous, but Beachy somehow knew he was on the right path. His mind was made up, and he was going to follow these men to Walla Walla himself and have them apprehended by local authorities.

As his wife fretted about his rash decision to leave unexpectantly, Beachy began preparing for his trip.

There are several valid reasons why Beachy should absolutely not have left Lewiston on a hunch:

1. He really could not afford to leave his two businesses, the Luna House and his stagecoach line.
2. He was not a policeman or lawman.
3. He really knew nothing about the killers, not even their real names, as they had checked in under false identities.
4. He didn't really know if Magruder was dead or alive.
5. He was also putting his own life in harm's way if these men really were cold-blooded killers.

But Beachy could not be persuaded to remain in Lewiston and do nothing except pray Magruder would eventually return safe and sound.

The next morning, as the killers got inside the stagecoach to head on their way, Beachy and Berry poked their heads into the wagon and demanded the

Hill Beachy's hotel and stage stop, the Luna House, in 1870. The building served as the courthouse from 1882 to 1889. *Courtesy of the Northwest Room, Spokane Public Library.*

men to show them their tickets. As they complied, Beachy and Berry both took a good hard look at the men's faces, burning them into their memories for future reference.

As the coach began to prepare for its departure, Beachy suddenly felt panic set in and quickly turned to his friend and said, "Please judge, I know Lloyd Magruder has been murdered, and the four men on that stage are his killers! Will you swear me in as a deputy and go with the sheriff and me to arrest them?"

Although the judge agreed that something did not sit right, he was still not assured that these men were killers. What tangible proof did they have? He reminded Beachy that Magruder's wife, Margaret, had just received a letter from him saying he would be back home in Lewiston in about twelve days. It was possible that Magruder's saddle was simply stolen, his plans delayed and/or he was experiencing trouble with his pack of mules.

But Beachy could not shake the dreaded feeling that his friend had been bludgeoned, no matter what the judge said to reassure him. In town, rumors began to circulate, and some folks thought that perhaps Beachy was losing his mind—it was only a dream after all. There was no real evidence that these men had actually killed Magruder.

So, against Beachy's desire, the carriage left in a trail of dust with the killers safely inside, leaving Beachy to figure out his next move. The coach would soon have a few hours' head start, valuable time lost when tracking criminals. After a quick prayer for guidance, Beachy kissed his wife goodbye, packed a bag and climbed aboard a stagecoach himself to travel the ninety long miles to Walla Walla.

Upon his arrival there, he found the men had already boarded a steamer that was headed to Portland, Oregon, via the Columbia River. Unwilling to give up his pursuit, he also slowly made his way to Portland. When he finally arrived in Oregon, much to Beachy's dismay, the men had already jumped another steamer that was heading to San Francisco, California.

As bad luck would have it, no other steamers were leaving Portland for San Francisco for another ten days.

It seemed the odds were against Beachy after all his hard work, time and travel—perhaps he was just being hasty and acting insane.

But then the nagging nightmare and the image of Magruger's bloody face would come back into his mind. No, he was sure he was correct in his theory.

With no other steamers leaving, he would have to be patient and think of a new plan. He did not have ten days to waste. Who knows where the men could hiding be in ten days. He quickly boarded another stagecoach that

The killers of Magruder and his crew fled Lewiston in a stagecoach similar to this one. *Courtesy of the Library of Congress, no. 2014681910.*

was heading to Yreka, California (at the time, Yreka was the only place close enough where one could secure telegraph services to San Francisco).

Once in Yreka, he jumped out of the coach and ran straight into the telegraph office. He quickly demanded that the telegraph operator send an urgent message to the head police officer in San Francisco, Chief Martin Burke, explaining the situation and demanding he apprehend the men and hold them in jail. Burke assigned the unusual case to detective Isaiah Lees, and it was decided that the criminals would be captured and detained as soon they came off the boat.

When the unsuspecting men disembarked the steamer, they were apprehended by the local authorities as planned. Beachy could relax for now.

But the justice system was as fallible then as it is now, and the killers were able to hire a fancy lawyer named Alexander Campbell (since they had a bunch of Magruder's gold dust to pay for his services), who filed a suit for a writ of habeas corpus, which basically demands prosecutors to "show the body" or the police could not detain the men.

Of course, there were no bodies to show, as the corpses had been hidden by the thugs miles away. Their lawyer also claimed that the California governor had no right to issue the warrant and outlined other legal technicalities, improper procedures, et cetera.

The determined Beachy refused to back down and demanded permission to extradite the men back to Idaho for a trial. After his long travels to capture these men, he would certainly not allow them to just go free. Beachy knew that if the men were not contained at this time, they would never find them again.

After much debate over procedures, Beachy was eventually granted the required permission to take the prisoners back to Idaho. So, the men were loaded up and carted back to Idaho to await their reckoning.

Upon arriving in Lewiston, they found a large and angry crowd had gathered, anxiously waiting for the killers to arrive so they could heckle them. For the safety of the prisoners, the criminals were kept upstairs, guarded by two strong men (and also heavily shackled with irons) in Beachy's hotel, the Luna House. Page, being innocent, was kept away from the other men, sitting alone in another room. The angry mob outside was not easily controlled, as they were understandably upset by the news of Magruder's gruesome murder.

When a reporter tried to take a photograph of the men who were arrested for the local paper, Lowery grabbed the instrument from his hands and threw it on the ground, breaking it into pieces. When the shocked reporter asked him why he did this, he oddly replied, "I thought it was loaded!" Lowery had obviously never seen a camera before and thought it was some sort of gun.

Page swore under oath that he took no part in the robbing and killing of Magruder, the others or his mules and offered to turn over evidence in order to help convict the assassins. He did state that he helped burn some evidence but said that he participated in that act only out of sheer fear. Truthfully, let's be honest, he had just witnessed his entire clan be bludgeoned to death. His testimony was crucial for the trial, as it secured that the three men had both opportunity and motive for the killings, plus Page had actually witnessed firsthand most of the brutal killings. Without much prodding, Page eagerly led the authorities back to the scene of the crime, where the bodies were hastily hidden. The corpses were still wrapped in the canvas tents in a pile down in the ravine, just as he had told the officers. The buried brass and iron fittings, however, were nowhere to be found.

After the trial, on the evening of January 23, 1864, the three men were found guilty and were scheduled to be hanged until their deaths on March 4.

The scaffold was erected in town at Judge Poe's house, and the three killers were walked up to their terrible (but well-deserved) fate of hanging from the gallows until their necks broke.

As the nose was tightened around Lowery's neck, he bizarrely said, "Launch your old boat; it's nothing but an old mud scow anyway!" (He had also left an obscene letter in his room to be read later.)

The *Evening Bulletin* in San Francisco stated: "In the whole record of crime, three murders more cold-blooded, instigated only by a lust for the hard-earned gold of others, can scarcely be found."

If Beachy had not acted on the premonition that came to him in a dream (even though many locals were making fun of him and questioning his sanity), would the killers of his best friend and other victims have ever been captured? Probably not. Beachy was a great man to be so strong and follow through with his hunch and bring punishment to these horrible and greedy good-for-nothing men!

Interesting Facts

- Beachy received $6,240 to reimburse him for his hard work and troubles.
- Page was later shot and killed by a man named Albert Igo, for reasons unknown, while visiting a house of prostitution
- Of the $25,000 stolen from Magruder, the $17,000 remaining, which was confiscated from the killers, was given to Caroline Magruder.
- The criminals' hangings were recorded as the first legal hangings in Idaho Territory.
- Beachy died of a stroke in San Francisco in 1875.
- In 1992, two men named Monty Spears and Tom Haugstad visited the murder site along the Nez Perce Trail with metal detectors. They were able to locate rusty harness buckles, nails and .33-caliber lead under a few inches of dirt, approximately where the bag of burned items was hidden. (Read the full article here: https://www.deseret.com/1992/8/17/19000457/artifacts-may-corroborate-evidence-from-1863-murder.)

Note: In 1980, the U.S. Forest Service named and maintains a 101-mile OHV dirt road, the Magruder Corridor, which runs through Idaho and Montana. This is the trail Magruder used on his fateful trip. At approximately mile marker 44.2 westbound (near the Selway River) is where Magruder's body was found.

1900: Tobacco Dealer Lies in a Pool of Blood

In the winter of 1900, a lone man named Matthew Mailey (also Mailley) was working late one night in his cigar and smoke shop in downtown Wallace. He both lived in and worked in his little shop in town. Everyone knew and liked Mailey.

But by the early hours of the next morning, the small town would be forever changed. When locals realized his store had not opened on time, they wondered why. Soon, people casually walking by his shop were horrified by what they saw as they peered through the plate-glass window.

Mailey's dead body was lying in a dark pool of blood near the rear of the small store. Some feared he may have died by suicide.

When the police arrived and carefully surveyed the scene, suicide was quickly ruled out. Mailey had suffered a crushed skull and slit throat. They found an eighteen-inch-long metal bar lying next to the body, covered in blood. Although people have been successful in carrying out suicide by slitting their throats or wrists, it would be hard for a person to commit suicide by hitting themselves with a bar. Especially impossible would be to hit oneself hard enough to crush one's own skull. At the time, the motive of robbery was not suspected, as the safe was still closed and locked and Mailey's corpse still had his watch on his person. Interestingly, the front door was locked, so whoever killed Mailey had the store key. They may have been an acquaintance or possibly worked there. No one knew of anyone who would have wanted to harm Mailey.

Police began to question locals to see if anyone saw or heard anything out of the ordinary. One witness said he saw Mailey enter his store around 6:00 p.m. the night before with a tall, thin unknown man. Another witness, an unnamed bartender in Wallace, said he had served a mysterious man a few shots of whiskey the evening of the murder and saw that he had fresh blood on his pants. When the bartender inquired about the blood on his trousers, the man did not have a valid answer as to the cause. He hurriedly downed his drink and then left the bar.

Curious, the bartender watched the stranger as he made his way to a nearby store and bought a fresh pair of paints.

The stranger hung around Wallace for the next couple of days, and he fluidly spent several hundred dollars in the small town. This frivolous spending caught the attention of the police. They also had another clue: the killer had put a handkerchief over the dead man's face after he killed him. This was a bad mistake, as the handkerchief had a laundry mark on it that

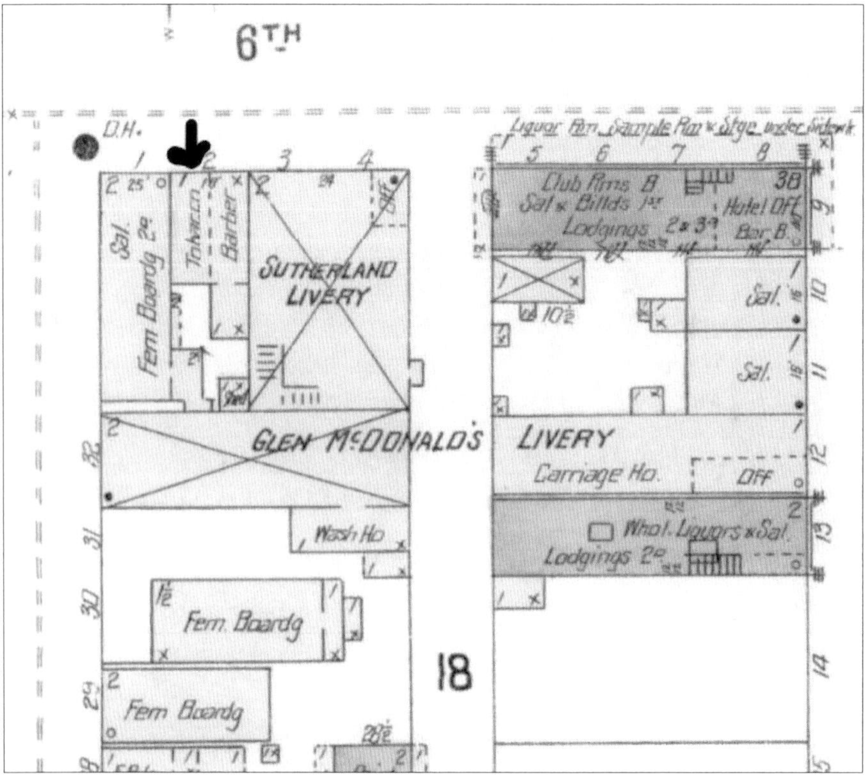

This Sandborn map from 1901 that (*arrow indicates*) possibly indicates the tobacco shop in Wallace, where Matthew Mailey was beaten to death with a metal bar that crushed his skull and his throat was slit. *Courtesy of the Library of Congress.*

connected the hanky to a man named Edward Rice. The officers thought that maybe Mailey was robbed as he was going to put the day's earnings into the safe, thus the safe was still locked.

When police cornered the stranger and questioned him, he confessed. He then told them that he had hidden the bloody pants behind the wainscoting in the room he was renting in Wallace. When he was arrested, he only had $2.60 in him, as he had squandered the rest of Mailey's hard-earned money.

Rice was promptly sent to the state penitentiary in Boise for the ruthless murder of Mailey.

While in jail, the other inmates did not like Rice and harassed him. They threatened him. Even though the guards thought he was amicable, the other prisoners wanted him dead.

After a trial found him guilty, Rice awaited his death by hanging. Even though Rice had confessed to the murder, his lawyer filed an appeal. The night before he was scheduled to hang, the appeal stayed his execution.

Although he should have been happy, this delay actually horrified Rice.

And for good reason. He knew the other inmates were eager to torture him.

Edward Rice was convicted of the brutal killing of Matthew Mailey. Before he was hanged to death, he said, "I do not think you are doing the right thing to put me out of the world." *Courtesy of the Idaho State Penitentiary and Ancestry.*

So that very night, Rice strategically hung his coat up in front of his bed to hide himself from the eyes of the guards. Suicidal, he quickly managed to slice his own throat with a sharp knife he had somehow secured. Two ten-inch-long gashes tore across his neck, severing his windpipe. The gurgling sounds from his cell finally caught the attention of the guards. As they looked inside his cell, they saw the gruesome sight of Rice bleeding everywhere. Before he slit his throat, he had smeared the word "nan" on the wall in his blood. What did "nan" mean?

A doctor was immediately summoned to the cell and determined that Rice would live. Under extreme protection from the guards, Rice slept through the night.

The next morning, Doctor Collister checked on the patient. He ordered a soft gruel to be cooked, and Rice was fed with some effort. It was curious how a man could slit his throat so violently two times and yet not sever either of his jugular veins. The doctor explained this to the men. As Rice threw his head back in the hopes of making the suicide more effective, he was actually doing the opposite. As he threw his head back, the movement caused the jugular veins to move tight across the neck bone, thus protecting them from the sharp blade.

When the doctor asked Rice why he had tried to commit suicide, with a scratchy voice Rice told his new story.

"Those men [the other prisoners] do not like me, and they have arranged to take me out tonight and hang me. I do not want to hang, yet I want to die. I am innocent!"

As Rice ate his gruel, he added, "What a cussed fool I have made of myself...but I am innocent."

His neck eventually healed, and Rice was kept under complete and strict supervision until the date of his execution. On November 30, 1901, a scaffold was erected, and Rice was led to the gallows. As he was being prepared for his death, Warden Arney said to the prisoner, "Goodbye." Rice smiled and said, "Goodbye, Mr. Arney," as if the two were old friends.

Right before they placed the black hood over his head and administered last rites, Rice was asked if he had any final words. He did.

"I have that about me which will protect me. I am afraid of no harm. I do not think you are doing the right thing to put me out of the world. There is lots of time," were Rice's final words on this Earth.

As the crowd of spectators huddling close eagerly gathered around the gallows to watch the man die, other citizens were shielded from the ugly sight by a thin muslin fabric strung around the scaffold.

At the exact hour, the lever was pulled, and Rice fell the five feet, five inches to his death. After a bit of twitching and with an arm flinging around a bit, his neck was finally broken, and Rice quit moving. The jail's physician checked the body for a pulse. There was none.

The physician then said to the crowd, "Ed Rice has paid the penalty for his crime that his soul, sin-stained and hardened, yet without immoral and perhaps repentant, at least not be judged by earthly judges, has been summoned by his maker."

Ed Rice was buried at the old Idaho State Penitentiary Cemetery.

A few questions remain long after Rice's death:

- One witness said they saw a tall, thin man entering the tobacco shop with Mailey the night before his murder. On the Idaho State Penitentiary description of convict records written during the time of his arrival, Rice's height was five feet, seven inches, and his weight was recorded at 183 pounds. Although that might seem somewhat "tall" during 1901, the weight of 183 would not be considered thin by any means.
- Rice was a known gambler, so he actually could have gotten lucky and won the money he was freely spending.
- He offered no explanation for the fresh blood on his pants. But why would he hide the pants and not just dispose of them? If he had come across a bunch of money, he could have afforded to just throw them away. It's strange.
- Mailey's skull was not only crushed, but the killer had also slit his throat. Why? One method or the other was sufficient to kill

A beautiful photograph of the tower at the Old State Penitentiary in Boise, Idaho. *Courtesy of Jeff Hitchcock, Flickr.*

the victim. Two types of attacks seem like overkill. Did Mailey have enemies? Why would his watch not be stolen?

- Why did Rice write the word "nan" on his wall when he attempted suicide? He never explained it. Was it part of a larger word?

Edward Rice, a notorious Shoshone County gambler, was hanged on Saturday morning, November 30, 1901. Did he really confess to the crime, or were the police just eager to have a killer in custody?

Only Mailey, Rice and God know the truth about what really happened that night inside Mailey's smoke shop.

1901: OFFICERS DOWN!

The tragic killing of police officers is one of the most senseless and heartbreaking murders of all. Men who have sworn to serve and protect often fall victim to the works of senseless and ruthless criminals.

On April 12, 1901, this was the case.

Two deputy sheriffs, Jim Rose and C.H. Williams, were patrolling the streets of Mullan, Idaho, when they were suddenly ambushed by three unseen assailants from behind. In the dark of the night, many shots were fired, and Deputy Williams began shooting back toward the location of the perpetrators. Tragically, Deputy Rose was shot three times.

Williams could hear the villains running away from the scene and into the blackness of the night. After he emptied his chamber, he returned to his partner's side.

Sheriff Sutherland was immediately summoned, and he and one of the brothers of the wounded, Deputy Frank Rose, quickly arrived at the bloody site. They had two bloodhounds with them.

As much as the hounds tried to pick up the scent of the scoundrels, their trail was cold.

The men decided to pick up the investigation again first thing in the morning.

As soon as daylight broke, the police were back at the shoot-out scene. About one hundred yards from where the officers thought the shots had come from, Sheriff Sutherland and Frank Rose found a gruesome surprise. The dead body of a man named Jack Powell was lying in the grass. Nearby, the officers found a cane, a hat and a revolver. Sutherland immediately recognized the revolver as one of his own. He had loaned the gun to one of his other deputies, a man named Pipkin, a few months earlier. Sutherland knew that Pipkin had been assaulted before the murders and that the gun had been stolen from him.

Sutherland looked down at the cold body of Jack Powell. Powell was an old-timer in Mullan, an ex–prize fighter and an all-around tough guy. He had been arrested earlier and had forfeited the revolver to cover his forty-five-dollar bail. He promptly fled to Montana to avoid any further prosecution.

No one even knew Powell had come back to Mullan until they discovered his body.

Thugs Paddy Rogers and Ben Smith were also arrested on suspicion of the crime.

1903: Wallace Opera House Cigar Murders

During a shoot-out at the opera house in Wallace on a cold November night in 1903, two men were wounded, and two others wound up dead. Why? Over smoking a cigar.

A grumpy old gentleman named William Cuff decided he wanted to smoke a cigar in the lobby of the opera house, but smoking was not allowed inside

The old opera house in Wallace, where William Cuff attacked two policemen because he was mad he could not smoke a cigar in the lobby in 1903. He was shot to death along with a bystander, Doctor Fims. *Courtesy of Amy Lynn of Wallace.*

the building. Officer Rose, a watchman for the theater, calmly approached Cuff and demanded he move outside to smoke or to please put out his cigar. This irritated Cuff greatly, and he stormed out of the building.

Rose thought that was going to be the end of it. But he was wrong.

Soon, the wonderful and enlightening theatrical performance by the James Neill Company was over, and elegantly dressed patrons began exiting the opera house. Pair by pair, they filed out onto the streets, enjoying the lovely evening, many possibly heading elsewhere for a night cap or a quiet stroll through town.

But the peaceful evening would soon take a turn for the worse.

Cuff quickly came out of the shadows and headed toward Rose in an excited manner. Rose caught the sight of a revolver in Cuff's right hand, but it was already too late. Cuff began shooting his gun at the chief of police McGovern and Officer Rose. Within seconds, both McGovern and Rose suffered personal injuries from the bullet wounds.

In retaliation, the wounded officers, Rose and McGovern, pulled their own guns and began firing back at Cuff. The frenzied crowd went wild and began running in all directions, fearing for their lives. As Cuff began running away himself, nearby unharmed policeman Quinn followed closely behind the assailant. He raised his gun and shot at Cuff four times, with three of the bullets penetrating him. Cuff died within seconds, his revolver on the ground beside his bloody body.

But the fourth bullet from Quinn's gun hit an innocent bystander named Dr. W.F. Fims in the head, killing him instantly. Fims was a well-respected local doctor and surgeon in the Silver Valley, and his death was a tragedy.

Perhaps Rose should have just allowed Cuff to puff away at his cigar.

1904: STEVE ADAMS AND HARRY ORCHARD: IDAHO'S RUTHLESS BAD BOYS

One of the most complicated and sensational trials from this era involved a local man named Steve Adams (1872–1934, also known as Steve Dixon), who finally got apprehended in the Coeur d'Alene region. He was tried three times for murder, and both of his Idaho murder trials ended in a hung jury. He was involved in so many crimes in multiple states (yet eventually was acquitted on all charges) that it is hard to keep track of them all. Many murders, attempted murders and violent acts were committed by him and one of his partners in crime, Harry Orchard (1866– 1954, his real name was Albert Horsley, but he was also known as Tom Hogan).

Adams and Orchard were notorious Idaho bad boys who had no problem with killing people.

Years went by that continually brought in new charges and accusations against Adams, involving him in everything from murders to dynamite explosions to the killing of ex–Idaho governor Steunenberg. But Adams always seemed to escape prosecution.

The labor wars in the region were getting worse by the minute. Many men, in support of the union miners, would go back and forth between Colorado and Idaho, causing havoc and killing nonunion mine workers. The amount of damage to property was overwhelming.

The long, complicated and bizarre trials against Steve Adams would begin and continue on for several years.

Adams would be implicated in:

- the murder of Fred Tyler;
- the murder of Ed Boule;

- involvement in the murder of ex-governor Frank Steunenberg;
- involvement in countless crimes in partnership with the notorious serial killer Harry Orchard (who eagerly and proudly confessed to dozens of murders);
- the murder of Lyle Gregory in Colorado;
- the murder of Arthur Collins;
- possible involvement in the murder of ex-sheriff Harvey Brown;
- the threatening of the life of Archie Phillips;
- involvement in the blowing up of the Independence Railroad Depot in Colorado that killed fourteen men;
- the failed assassination attempt of General Wells;
- and so many other crimes.

As a member of the Western Federation of Miners, Adams had trials that became very complicated, and his defense attorneys went to great lengths to get him acquitted on all charges. Adams was basically a very dangerous arson, a sociopath and serial killer. Yet in his mind, he thought he was doing it for the "good of the union," but in reality, the Western Federation of Miners was just using him as a pet dog. His many trials were intertwined on so many levels that it is hard to follow.

Harry Orchard was guilty of almost twenty murders, including the killing of ex–Idaho governor Frank Steunenberg in 1905. *From Wikimedia Commons, public domain.*

Strangely, even with all the witnesses and multiple charges that piled up against him, Adams would eventually be set free. How and why is beyond comprehension. The Western Federation of Miners footed the bill for Adams, manipulating him every which way it could to get whatever testimony it needed from him at the time.

But Adams was used as a puppet for the Western Federation of Miners, and (when they were done using him) they dropped him cold turkey. And as soon as the big case against Moyer was dismissed, the organization quickly lost all interest in Adams. He was genuinely confused by this. While he was in jail in Colorado, no one visited him—not even his wife.

The details of Adams's and Orchard's crimes are both complicated and fascinating.

The First Known Murder: Arthur Collins, Telluride, Colorado, November 19, 1902

Arthur Collins was a thirty-year-old man and the manager of the Smuggler-Union Mine in Telluride, Colorado. During the Colorado Labor Wars, he was not liked by some of the miners, as he had cut their wages and minimized some of their safety measures in order to increase profit. These greedy changes cost twenty-four men their lives, as a fire broke out in the mine in 1901. The changes made work conditions very unsafe.

A labor strike formed and was backed by the Western Federation of Miners. All the men were demanding was a unified workday at a minimum wage. Their hours were long, sometimes fourteen-hour shifts, for three dollars a day. Some even had to purchase their own dynamite for the job.

Superintendent Collins, although was well liked and respected in the community, was starting to get a bad reputation from the miners who worked under him. When he decided to go ahead and reopen the Smuggler-Union Mine with nonunion men, it did not go over well with the mine workers.

In retaliation, the leaders of the Western Federation of Miners quickly purchased 250 rifles and 50,000 rounds of ammunition on July 3, 1901. In an act of revenge, one night, as the "scabs" (nonunion people who cross picket lines to work) were leaving the mine after a long shift, hidden union men opened fire on them. As the scabs scattered, many were wounded, and one man was killed instantly. (Since the shoot-out went on for a long time, it is surprising that more men were not killed.)

The scabs quickly surrendered, but even after that, the miners marched them up the side of a hill and continued to beat them up or shoot at them. The entire ambush was horrific.

When the strike officially ended on November 9, 1902, the miners' pay back to Collins came that same night.

While Collins and a few of his buddies were gathered together playing cards, an unknown person fired shots at 9:00 p.m. through a window and into the house where the men were seated. The buckshot shattered through Collins's body, and he jumped up, yelling, and then fell to the floor in a bloody heap. His liver, stomach and kidneys were instantly destroyed. His children and wife had to watch the disaster and Collins's murder.

During the Collins trial, eight people testified that Adams was nowhere near the scene of the crime. They stated that Adams was with them, innocently playing cards at Mrs. Mennan's Boarding House in Ophir the night Collins was shot (November 19, 1902). They also said Adams was still there the next morning when news of the murder reached them. Whether this story is true or just a fake alibi, the world will never know.

The killer was never identified or captured. Some were determined it was the work of Harry Orchard and Steve Adams; others said it was an angry scab whom Collins did not protect from the ambush. It is hard to tell, and the killer never confessed, of course. Later (in 1908, when he was finally being tried for the crime), Adams would fear for his life, because he knew if he was acquitted, Colorado citizens would lynch him themselves.

The Murder of Detective Lyle Gregory: May 1904

Two years after the fact, Adams was arrested on a fugitive warrant for the murder of Lyle Gregory by Attorney Kolesch via a telegram from Colorado. Gregory was a detective and special agent. On his way home from Edward Cleary's Saloon in West Denver late at night, Gregory was shot down while walking in an alley. Complete overkill, ten bullets had been fired into his body. Just weeks earlier, he had been getting death threats and was assaulted by William Warjon. On September 11, 1906, Governor McDonald requested Adams be extradited to Colorado for the trial concerning the murder of Gregory.

The Murder of Fourteen Men: June 6, 1904

All the details about the blowing up of the Independence Railroad Depot in Colorado are unclear. Adams and his partner in crime Harry Orchard were known dynamite junkies. The horrific explosion instantly killed fourteen nonunion men and was completed through orders that came from the leaders of the Western Federation of Miners in retaliation. Orchard and Adams placed two boxes of dynamite under the depot the night before. To establish an alibi, they went camping nearby. As the other men slept, Orchard and Adams rode their horses down to the depot, placed the dynamite and rode back and slept. This way, when everyone arose and saw the two men fast asleep, they would have an air-tight alibi.

Early the next morning, as the nonunion men began boarding the train to take them to work, Orchard set off the bomb. Tragically, thirteen of the twenty-seven men were killed instantly, body parts strung all over the depot.

Another man died later from his wounds, and six men were saved only by amputating their arms and/or legs.

The miners were working for three dollars a day during a ten-hour shift.

The Murder of Fred Tyler: August 8, 1904

The fall of 1904 turned up the gruesome, cold-blooded and very complicated murder of Fred Tyler over a timber claim near Coeur d'Alene, which the other men felt he had jumped. The killers, Steve Adams, Alvin Mason and Jack Simpkins, hung out together in a small cabin hidden in the woods. Angry about the jumping of the timber claim, Simpkins willingly paid Adams $120 to kill Tyler. Claim jumping was a very risky and often fatal move for the jumper. In both mineral and lumber claims, a jumper was one who illegally occupied property that another person legally had the right to, much in the same manner a property "squatter" operates today by illegally living in a house someone else legally owns. Adams seemed to be involved in punishing both timber and mine claim jumpers.

In the 1900s, jumping a claim was certain death, but many still tried.

Fred Tyler had decided to take that risk, which proved fatal. Tyler had come to the area the previous year for work. The rumor was that a man named Gus Chruestein had given Tyler the claim, but apparently, there were no records of this transaction.

When the legal owners of the claim found out, they decided they would have to come up with a plan to get rid of any jumpers.

So, the men decided to go on a friendly fishing trip together. After fishing, the men took Tyler back to the cabin in the woods to stay overnight. Tyler knew he had been had. The night lingered on, and Tyler must have spent the evening absolutely terrified, knowing of his impending death.

The next morning at 5:00 a.m., they made Tyler walk deep into the woods, and as Tyler had his back to the other men, Adams shot him in the head in cold blood. The men tried to hide the body in between some logs and then quickly covered his body with a burlap sack.

Coldly, they walked back to the cabin as if nothing had ever happened.

A few miles away, Archie Phillips (a friend of Tyler's and an enemy of the Simpkins/Adams gang) was just waking up when he heard the shots fired in the woods. Just weeks earlier, a man named Boule's body had been found just thirty feet from Simpkin's cabin, so Phillips was on guard.

The last day Tyler's mother saw her son was May 31, and he was thirty-four years old at that time. Tyler was considered missing as of August 10. During the lengthy trial, Tyler's mom was asked why she didn't go view his body or even go to the burial. She was also asked why she did not dress properly while in mourning. Her only answer was that she could not afford new clothes, as she did not have the money. One would think that if the Western Federation of Miners was paying Adams's entire attorney bill, they could have bought the poor mother of one of the victims a dress.

For unknown reasons, a week after they killed Tyler, the guilty party went to the sheriff to give notice that he was "missing."

Apparently, Adams confessed to the murder to a detective and was arrested. Sheriff Sutherland wanted Adams released on a writ of habeas corpus. Harry Orchard had told police that his friend (Adams) and Simpkins killed Tyler and was his accomplice in multiple murders.

Adams's first trial was held in Wallace in February 1906. He was moved from the state penitentiary in Boise to Wallace to be tried for murder. Simpkins was still a fugitive from justice and missing in action. Adams confessed by signature this time to the murder of Tyler and for a number of other crimes committed with Harry Orchard.

Then he quickly renounced his confession, as he asserted that Pinkerton agents and Detective McParland offered him immunity if he confirmed Harry Orchard's claims.

One of the problems with the Tyler trial was that Tyler's body could not be definitively identified. D.E. Keyes, the coroner for the case, was also in trouble. On the stand, he was asked why he never held a formal inquest over Tyler's remains, which were found on July 26, 1905.

On the stand, Keyes was asked by defense council, Clarence Darrow, "You knew did you not that the law requires an inquest to be held when a body is discovered and there is suspicion of foul play?"

Keyes muttered a quiet, "Yes."

"Did you send out for any witnesses after you received the bones?'

"No."

"Why?"

Keyes faltered, "Because the state suggested that it was impossible to hold an inquest where the bones were found, if not enough inhabitants are in the immediate vicinity where the body was found, to constitute a coroner's jury. That's one reason. Another is that no one seemed to know anything about the body except as relative to identification."

The coroner's reasoning seems sketchy.

Among Tyler's remains was a bottle of horseradish. This was key in identifying the remains. The horseradish was identified as the same supply given to Tyler by Mrs. Phillips the day before his fishing trip and disappearance. The horseradish was found near the corpse in his fishing bag.

Much to the dismay of Tyler's friends and family, his skeleton was brought into the courtroom to be exhibited for the jury.

Jacob Yeager was called to try to identify the body, as he had known Tyler for nine years. He said he knew it was Fred because of the shape of the skull, the color of the hair, his calloused feet, the crooked finger and the shoes found nearby.

During trial, Tyler's extremely distraught mother identified her son's body by the joint on his little finger. It was crippled due to a baseball injury when he was young. The calloused feet, she explained, were from being severely frost bitten a few years before. In her distress, she pulled out a photograph of her son and demanded the juror's look at it.

Darrow, Adams's attorney, objected to her actions, stating, "One cannot prove the identity of a man whose skeleton alone is produced by a photo taken of him while alive!"

Captain C.A. Waters, the oldest man on the jury and a prominent old-timer in Coeur d'Alene, showed signs of sympathy for the grieving mother.

As much as the positive identity of the remains caused problems for the jurors, the actual date of the murder began bouncing around, which could nullify Adams's guilt.

- A man named Orville Mason was hauling hay up the river earlier that year and told the jury that Adams was helping him. The entire Alvin Mason family testified that they saw Adams at a family birthday party on August 7 and that Adams continued to work for Mason until around August 8. Newton Glover and Steve Adams were the only other people there aside from the family. Defense attorneys tried to get the date of Tyler's murder changed from August 10 to August 7. The reason? Because this would mean that Adams could not have killed Tyler on August 7 and that it was possible Mason was the one who shot him.
- Tyler ate supper at the Phillipses' home (and thus given the horseradish) on August 6, so he must have been murdered on August 7. The scene of the crime was fifteen miles away. The shots were heard at 5:00 a.m., so there was no way Adams could have gotten back to Mason's cabin for dinner.

- Adams was helping haul hay with Orville Mason on August 7 and 8. He was then logged as leaving the cabin and headed out to Coeur d'Alene on August 8, and he stayed in a cheap hotel in Spokane. Four days after Bouley was murdered, Adams went to Denver.
- Tyler was in Coeur d'Alene on August 10.
- Tylers body was never officially identified.
- When Darrow asked Adams, "Did you kill Tyler?" He replied flatly, "No."

The *Coeur d'Alene Press* printed part of Adams's gruesome confession to the murder of Tyler on November 12, 1907:

> *The next day, Simpkins and I went up to the claim and met some settlers called Mason and Newt Glover, who had a crooked eye. There was also a man running a store, who was called Price, who seemed to be a friend of Simpkins. There were some jumpers there, and it seemed as if they were trying to take claims from the settlers, and Simpkins said if I would help get rid of the jumpers, he would give me $300. I agreed in carrying out the agreement, and two of the men were killed. Mason and Glover were with me when the first man was killed, but Mason did not do any of the killings. The man was Tyler, and he was killed by a shot from a .25-35 Winchester. Simpkins was at Wardner at the time, but Mason, Glover and myself went to Simpkins's claim. He was gone, so we lay until the sun went down, but he did not return. We went up to the spring, and as we were drinking, we heard him* [Tyler] *coming, and I said, "I am glad of it." I got my Winchester and stood by the side of the trail and told him to throw up his hands. He had a big gun buckled on, and we disarmed him and took him to Simpkins's cabin, kept him there all night. Then took him out three miles out in the timber next day and killed him. We placed his body between two logs. Tyler had told that he had been placed on the claim by a lumberman of Spokane named Lewis, but I am not sure about that.... Well, after a while, we will go back and get the rest of them fellers on the other claims.*

Even with all the evidence and Adams's confession, the jury could not agree and gave Judge Wood their outcome: eight acquitted him, and four wanted a conviction. Sheriff Bailey of Wallace came to Coeur d'Alene and stood by with a warrant for Adams's arrest for the murder of Bouley.

Clarence Darrow was an aggressive and high-profile attorney in Coeur d'Alene and the Silver Valley. *From the* Coeur d'Alene Press, *November 11, 1907.*

Attorney Clarence Darrow announced to the press, "We expected a verdict of not guilty but of course are not absolutely cast down by the result."

What other men was Adams planning on killing? Who was the second man besides Tyler he spoke of killing? Was he speaking about Ed Bouley, another jumper whose body was found a week after Tyler's? No clarification can be found.

The Murder of Ed Bouley: Mid-August 1904

The body of another man, Ed Bouley (or Boules), was discovered by a local sheriff just thirty feet from Simpkins's cabin in the woods near Coeur d'Alene. He had five shots buried in his body. When Frank Price testified during this trial in 1907, he told the jury that he rushed to the river the day Bouley was killed and yelled out to Mason that he was dead. Supposedly, Mason just called back, "I am glad Bouley was killed." And later, "Ed Bouley is dead, and everyone in that settlement rejoiced."

Supposedly, Adams was given $300 in cash to kill Bouley.

Sheriff Bailey of Wallace came to Coeur d'Alene and stood by with a warrant for Adams's arrest for the murder of Bouley.

Just before his murder, Bouley told his attorney on July 19, "If he should get me before I return, you can bring me back and plant me on my claim."

When his attorney asked him, "Who is *he*?" Bouley just said, "The president of the Claim Jumpers Killing Association!"

Apparently, Bouley foretold his looming death.

A man who somehow defied his own death, N. Lindsey, was with Bouley when he was killed. His story is chilling:

> *Bouley and I were claim jumpers. We were at the creek getting water. Bouley was stooping over to get a drink when I heard a gun, and he fell over onto me. I ran for the trees, and while running, a bullet struck me in the arm. Not a soul could be seen anywhere, the shots coming from the thick brush. From behind a tree, I saw fifteen more bullets being pumped into Bouley's prostrate body.*

Trouble had been brewing for months. Squatters had become popular in the region, due to the fact that they desired to get first filing rights when the land was officially surveyed. Timber was at an all-time-high demand and had a high value.

Tyler's body had been found earlier in the same place Bouley's body was found.

Several locals had theories about these two murders.

The first theory is that Lindsey and Bouley were the real killers of Tyler. After they committed the murder, they fought over the crime, which caused Lindsey to also kill Bouley.

The second theory is that a jealous man, Frank Price (who ran the nearby grocery store), killed Bouley because he was sleeping with his wife. When Price was asked about Bouley's death, he calmly said, "It's all right. It saved me from killing him."

Bouley was a well-known but not liked timber claim jumper. Sheriff Charles Manley felt sure that Bouley's death was caused by claim jumping and not a jealous husband. The police had found a coat behind some logs that belonged to a man who headed the secret meetings against squatters, a group that swore to actively kill any and all claim jumpers on the spot.

Manley told the *Coeur d'Alene Press* the grisly details on August 27:

> *Although we had the coroner with us, we didn't hold any formal inquest. We found the body just where the murder occurred. Nobody had disturbed it. It had four bullet holes in it: two in the face and head, one in the shoulder*

and one in the back. Bouley was lying on his back, and every circumstance showed his murderers turned him over after killing him and shot him in the back. We found one .30-30 cartridge and one .25-30 cartridge on the scene of the murder....On the trail near where Bouley was shot, we found his horse and dog. Both had been shot, too. Lindsey said the assailants had also tried to shoot him. Bouley was buried in a shallow trench where he was shot. Decomposition had already set in when we arrived, making it impossible to bring the body out. I am convinced that Bouley was killed by squatters. There have been several angry and secret meetings of the squatters since jumpers went in there in May. And from what I am told, assassination and murder have been openly discussed.

George Bruun was also later questioned and suspected of the murder. When the police caught up with him, they discovered that Bruun was nowhere in the vicinity when Bouley was shot.

He told the *Coeur d'Alene Press* on August 27, "Last Wednesday, I was out on a trail near my house when I met my little boy going to the neighbor's house. He said, 'Mama is sending me there on an errand.' I went and found my wife and Bouley, who is now dead, sitting on the bed together. Bouley jumped up and ran out the back door, and my wife commenced to crying."

He obviously had good motive to kill Bouley.

When asked about the murdering of claim jumpers, he said, "I was invited to the meetings [to get rid of jumpers] because, while I myself was a squatter, too, I was under suspicion of selling goods to the jumpers....They wanted to know if they should hang the jumpers, shoot them or tar and feather them." Bruun and his wife broke up, and she made her way to Coeur d'Alene to spend time with her friends before moving on.

In 1907, Adams finally came clean about the activities involving Bouley's murder. The *Coeur d'Alene Press* printed part of Adams's gruesome confession on November 12, 1907:

A week later [after Tyler was killed], *we went back and met a fellow named Bouley and another man near Simpkins's cabin. Simpkins and me and Glover and another man opened fire on Bouley and another fellow, and we killed Bouley. The second man dodged about, and we missed him. I went down to Glover's ranch and waited until the sheriff from Wallace had made an investigation, and then we went back and burned up all the jumpers' cabins except one. There were two or three of them* [victims] *anyway. The sheriff only found Bouley's body and that right in front*

> *of Simpkins's cabin, but he did not accuse Simpkins as far as I know. Simpkins did not give me the $300. He said that all the settlers had agreed to help pay it but did not come in with the money. I got $100 from Mason and $20 from Simpkins. I think there was a rich man up here trying to rob these people of their claims. This was the man Lewis and Tyler told me that he was to furnish the money to hold them up there on their claims until they could take them away from the settlers, and then he was to give them half and he would keep the other half. The claims had good timber on them. I went back to Denver and did not go to do the Steunenberg job because they had not sent the money, and I was not going down there broke....I waited for three to four weeks and then went on to Denver.*
>
> *They did not tell me how much there was in it for me, but there was an understanding beforehand that I was to get $1,000 a job. I was not supplied with how the job was to be done....He said as soon as we got rid of the jumper, we would go down and get Steunenberg out of the way.*

They also wanted to get rid of Steunenberg because of the stand he took in regard to the Coeur d'Alene strike. Deep down, Adams knew the Western Federation of Miners used him as a tool in the hopes that the reign of terror from several of the cases would end.

When Archie Phillips was questioned about Bouley's death, he said, "As Tyler and I went down the creek fishing one day, about a week before, we saw Adams and Simpkins on the trail. As we sat there, twelve shots were fired overhead in Bouley's direction and believed he was killed."

Attorney Darrow said the jury, "Turn him loose if you will—if you think it is right—and you will be turning loose a red-handed murderer to prey on other people again and bathe his hands in innocent blood!"

Even with all the evidence and Adams's confession, the jury could not agree and gave Judge Wood their outcome: eight acquitted him, and only four wanted a conviction.

Adams and Harry Orchard in the Winter of 1904 in Denver

Both men were encountering financial problems and were living in poverty. Apparently, Adams was free from jail for a brief stint. Orchard told the *Coeur d'Alene Press* on June 12, 1907, that he and Adams were so hungry that winter, they had to resort to stealing sheep from a local farmer's fields in order to eat.

Witness Against the Moyer/Haywood/Pettibone Case in the Murder Trial of Idaho's Ex-Governor Frank Steunenberg

Adams was also a key witness in the trial against Moyer/Haywood/Pettibone for the murder of Idaho's ex-governor Frank Steunenberg. Adams was a crucial witness for the state against Haywood (an alleged participant in the murder). Notorious killer and bomb builder Harry Orchard had no problem explaining to the police that he and Adams were friends and that Adams was his partner in the assassination of Steunenberg. He also told the officers that Adams was his partner in many other "bumping off" expeditions. Orchard did not disclose exactly how many people they had bumped off.

Murder of Idaho's Ex-Governor Frank Steunenberg 1905

The horrible death of Idaho's ex-governor Frank Steunenberg (1861–1905) by Steve Adams and Harry Orchard (1866–1954) left a deep scar on Idaho's history.

Convicted killer Harry Orchard (whose real name was Albert Horsley) went to prison for almost fifty years for his crimes. There, he grew strawberries and tended to the chickens for the penitentiary. *From the* Gem State Rural, *April 1, 1908.*

On a cold night on December 30, 1905, a homemade bomb exploded at the gate to the ex-governor's home, blowing him to pieces.

In Idaho, Harry Orchard was a well-known assassin and terrorist. Steve Adams and Harry Orchard both testified in 1907 that the man responsible for initiating and financing the murder of Governor Frank Steunenberg was Haywood himself. They had to get involved in the killing because of a botched attempt previously made by Orchard and Jack Simpkins.

Orchard was mad at Steunenberg because he believed he would have become a wealthy mine owner if Steunenberg hadn't forced him out of Idaho.

Harry Orchard had no problem using dynamite to get his point across. He could remain completely unemotional and detached as he created extreme destruction all around him. He felt no concern over killing an innocent victim or two in the process.

Under Orchard's belt was a long list of other crimes he confessed to committing with or without Steve Adams in tow. He claimed all of these actions were inspired and demanded by Haywood. The other side argued that the men's stories were just false claims about murders and mysteries told by Sheriff James McParland and the Pinkerton detectives in order to lead to the conviction of the leaders of the Western Federation of Miners.

Harry calmly gave a list of his crimes to the detectives:

- He calmly lit one of the fuses that blew up the Bunker Hill and Sullivan Mine.
- He built a bomb to destroy the Vindicator Mine at Cripple Creek and killed two men named McCormick and Beck in 1903.
- He murdered Martin Gleason, the manager of the Wild Horse Mine, in Colorado in 1901.
- He murdered J.W. Barney in 1901 and Wesley J. Smith in 1902, bosses at the Smuggler-Union Mine in Telluride, Colorado.
- He murdered Frank Herne.
- He burned down a cheese factory in Ontario in order to secure the $800 insurance claim. (Orchard said he began his life of crime by selling cheese at a short weight and keeping the profit.)
- He planted a bomb at the gate of Judge Goddard in Denver, Colorado.
- He fired buckshot into the body of Detective Lyle Gregory in Denver, killing him.
- He stalked Governor Peabody and Judge Gabbert in Denver, waiting for the opportunity to kill them both.
- He planned the blowing up of the railway station at the Independence Mine at Independence, Colorado, that killed fourteen men in 1904.
- He hired a man to poison a former associate named Nelville, who was going to testify against him in the trial concerning the Independence job.
- He blew up an electric powerhouse in Colorado in 1905.
- He failed his attempt to blow up Chief Judge Gabbart of Colorado, which did kill an innocent bystander.
- He attempted to kill Fred Bradley (an executive in the Bunker Hill and Sullivan Mine) while he was living in San Francisco by putting strychnine into his milk when it was left at his door. This plot failed, so in November 1904, he arranged a bomb, which

blew Bradley into the street when he opened his door in the morning and destroyed his house.
- He murdered Arthur Collins in Telluride with partner in crime, Steve Adams.
- He attempted to kill General Sherman Bell multiple times.
- He murdered Dave Moffat.
- He murdered Idaho's ex-governor Frank Steunenberg.

When Orchard was convicted, he told the detectives his life story—some true and some fiction. He told them that after traveling all around the states, in 1897, he settled down at Wallace, Idaho, where he became a milk delivery man. He watched the tension get worse every day between the union miners and the management in the Coeur d'Alenes. Orchard saw the tension as a way to make a profit. He would travel and participate in violent protests and was eager to make bombs if needed (as he did for the Vindicator Mine in Colorado).

Orchard and his pals just could not stay clear of trouble. In Denver, they approached a man who was working for a local mine company who had been known to harass and assault men in the United Miner Workers of America. It was reported that Orchard and his friend Bill Haywood went back to their lodge and grabbed a sawed-off shotgun. They then followed the man, and when he stopped in an alley, Haywood filled him with lead.

In 1905, the vicious gang of Charles Moyer, Bill Haywood, George Pettibone and Harry Orchard gathered to devise the plot to kill the ex-governor Steunenberg. Haywood even gave Orchard $300 for travel expenses. Orchard made his way from Denver to Portland and Seattle and then finally to Caldwell, Idaho, where he began his search for Steunenberg's home. Once he located the home, Orchard devised a horrific plan to blow up Steunenberg at his residence in Caldwell, Idaho. (He later confessed his dreadful plan to Pinkerton Agents James McParland and George Hueber).

The story of the assassination is sketchy, and truthfully, how much the other three men were involved in the murder is unknown. Newspaper stories vary. Who was the mastermind behind the plot? Orchard? The other men? All of them?

Orchard stalked Steunenberg and wrote down his daily movements and schedules. Steunenberg frequented Boise on business and stayed at the Idanha Hotel. Orchard wanted to place a bomb under his bed in his room at the Idanha to blow him up, but he quickly abandoned the idea and developed another one he liked better.

Orchard decided to go to Steunenberg's home on Christmas Eve to shoot him through the window, but again, he changed his mind.

He settled on his final idea. He would build a bomb and place it on the outside gate of the Steunenberg residence. When the gate was opened, the bomb would explode, killing Steunenberg instantly.

So on the snowy, blistery day of December 30, 1905, the unsuspecting ex-governor went for a walk. Upon his return, he approached the wooden gate attached to his side door. As he pulled the slide and swung the gate open, the bomb exploded at 1602 Dearborn Street in Caldwell.

As he lay on the ground in a bloody pulp, Steunenberg's last words were, "They finally got me." He meant the Western Federation of Miners finally "got him."

Steunenberg was soon dead.

Orchard walked back to his hotel and made no attempt to flee from the crime scene. He went on with his life as usual, playing cards and drinking. Back at the Saratoga Hotel in Caldwell, one observant waitress noticed Orchard was noticeably trembling. The police eventually became suspicious of him for the murder of Steunenberg. When the police searched his room, no. 19, at the Saratoga Hotel they found incriminating evidence, including pieces of bomb fragments on a desk and chunks of plaster of Paris in his chamber pot.

He tried to clear his name, but to no avail. He was finally arrested on the murder charge. He eventually confessed to the bombing, seeming almost proud. He also ratted out Charles Moyer, Bill Haywood and George Pettibone (and included Jack Simpkins, a Western Federation of Miners committee member) for their involvement in the plot, saying they paid him to kill Steunenberg.

Charles Darrow was hired to defend Haywood, Moyer and Pettibone, and since the prosecutor was unable to present any information against the men, they were acquitted by the jury. Orchard did not get so lucky. During the three-month-long trial, it was discovered that Orchard had a second motive for killing Steunenberg. He continually blamed Steunenberg for screwing up his plans to make a bunch of money in the mining industry.

Simpkins was nowhere to be found, and the Pinkerton Agency offered a $2,000 reward for him, and anyone with information was to call the Spokane agency at phone number 234.

During his trial, Orchard endured thirty-two and a half hours of examinations. He left the stand finally at 2:30 p.m., after he had identified the casing of the bomb he had built and used at Judge Goddard's home in Denver, Colorado.

In June 1907, Orchard confessed to his sins during a cross-examination conducted by Detective McParland. He noted that tough guy Orchard began rocking and crying. Orchard said he wanted to come clean and make all possible reparations by offering his confession.

The *Coeur d'Alene Press* printed his confession:

> *I thought of putting myself out of the way* [suicide], *but I thought over my past life. I did not believe in the hereafter at all, but I was afraid to die and thought of all the times that I have been such a monster. Many of my crimes had been so great that I would not be forgiven. I had been sent a Bible and read it and came to the conclusion that I would be forgiven if I made a confession of everything, and I made up my mind to tell the truth.*

Orchard was sentenced to forty-six years at the Idaho State Penitentiary in 1908, although he was originally sentenced to hang on May 15 that year. Harry Orchard, because he had provided evidence against the other men, received life imprisonment rather than the death penalty. He confessed to killing no less than twenty-one men. He was offered immunity for his crimes for giving evidence against the Western Federation of Miners.

When he was offered parole years later, Orchard declined the offer. He said he would rather live out his days within the confines of the prison, which he did until his death in 1954.

Later, Adams wrote a confession about the Steunenberg murder that was printed in the *Coeur d'Alene Press* on November 12, 1907:

> *I am a member of the Western Federation of Miners.... While I worked in Colorado, I became acquainted with Charles Moyer, William Haywood and George Pettibone shortly after the assassination of Arthur Collins in Telluride, Colorado, and have been intimately acquaintance with them ever since I left Denver. I have had conversations with them regarding the assassination of Governor Steunenberg, and they told me to go see Jack Simpkins at Wardner. This conversation took place shortly after the dynamiting of the depot at Independence in 1904, in the backroom of Pettibone's store. Haywood was present, and they told me to go see Simpkins, as he would probably tell me about the Steunenberg matter, as they wanted to get Steunenberg. Moyer was not present. I think he was in jail at Telluride. They gave me $200 to go up to Idaho.... They did not give me any direction as to how to remove Steunenberg, but it was understood that I was to use my own judgement. I left Denver, went to Wallace, then to*

The prison cell blocks inside the old Boise State Penitentiary. *Courtesy of Eric Friedebach.*

> *Burke....I returned to Wallace on July 4th, went down to Wardner to meet Simpkins. Simpkins was in bed, and I talked to him through the window. We arranged to meet in the morning, and at breakfast, we would talk of the Steunenberg matter. Simpkins said he would write and get some money, and we would go down together on the Steunenberg case. He wrote for the money, but I don't know whether or not he got it.*

Booked into the Boise Idaho State Penitentiary: February, 20, 1906

Steve Adams went to the state penitentiary in late February; his inmate number was 1203. He was being held for the trial concerning his complicity in the assassination of Frank Steunenberg on December 30, 1905. In his "Description of Convict" file, there was very little information other than the fact that Adams had $4.55 on him, and his possessions were listed as the cash, a coat and a watch. Strangely, his personal information, such as height, weight, marks, religious affiliation, living relatives, et cetera, are all absent from his convict card. Why?

Personal Letter Written to His Family: March 3, 1906

Spring brought about Adams's desire to communicate with his family. After he was booked into the state penitentiary, he began receiving letters from his aunt and uncle. This was the heartfelt and brutally honest handwritten letter he wrote back to them:

> *Mr. and Mrs. Oliver, my dear aunt and uncle, I received your most welcome letter and was glad to hear from you all and of your belief in my innocence. I wish to God that I was, but I fell in with bad company and was led to commit a number of most vile sins, breaking the law of both man and God. Had I stayed with my church and with the raising of my parents, who are, I believe, in Heaven, I would be a free man today, but I allowed myself to be led into sin most damnable. I am going to try to undo what I have done and do no more. I expect that when my friends find out the real truth, they will disown me, but God knows I could not help it. I hope you all pray for me and my forgiveness. I am going to just tell you the facts in this case and others and put my trust in God to guide me through it. If I can do some good the rest of my life, I am willing to try. I think is all a poor sinner can do when he has sinned so bad. As to your basket, it will be very thankfully received. The warden treats me very kindly. I have plenty to eat and a god place to sleep. I have a little baby boy almost three months old named after my poor father, David. Auntie, don't forget to pray for me. I feel the disgrace of my sins very sharply. I have 480 acres in Oregon. I had my wife and babies out with my friends so people would not bother them to death. She feels very bad. I am sure I asked her to pray for me, too. She is the best woman in the world. It nearly kills me to think of the misery I have caused her, which I will never cause again. Excuse a short letter. When people find out all the facts in these cases, I hope they will forgive me. Hoping to hear from you all soon. I will close with my love to you all. Your nephew, Stephen Adams. Direct in care of the warden, Penitentiary, Boise, Idaho.*

The Transportation of Adams Back to Wallace: August 18, 1906

Moving Adams from the state penitentiary in Boise to Moscow to Wallace for another trial was a huge undertaking. In the custody of Shoshone County sheriff Angus Sutherland, Adams should have felt safe, but he must have known more than he was letting on, because the entire trip, he was a nervous wreck and was constantly looking over his shoulder. Did he fear for his life? Did he receive death threats like so many others?

The men traveled on horseback from Moscow to Lovell, where they boarded a train that took them the rest of the way to Wallace, where he was finally tried for the murder of Fred Tyler. The entire trip, Adams was in great fear. Sutherland did not know why.

When the men arrived in Moscow, some attention was quickly drawn to their arrival. After a brief dinner, Sutherland ordered, "Have the best four-horse team in the barn here in twenty minutes! Give me a drive that has knowledge of the road and abundance of nerve!"

Mr. Byrnes, the stable keeper, calmly told the sheriff, "I'll send Larry Burk with you. The word *fear* is not in his dictionary."

The prisoner, Sheriff Sutherland and two other fully armed officers and the armed driver set off on the long trip from Moscow to Wallace, about seventy miles. At Wallace, Detectives McParland and Thiel, state penitentiary warden E.L. Whitney and attorney Leon Witsell (also defense attorney in the Moyer/Haywood/Pettibone case) were all waiting eagerly for Adams's arrival. It had been decided that if Adams was not convicted of Tyler's murder and was released, he would immediately be arrested by a Colorado deputy and taken back to Colorado to await trial for the murder of Detective Lyte Gregory (murdered May 14, 1904).

The men were again up to no good and were planning on placing a huge dynamite bomb underneath a boardinghouse in Denver that held 150 nonunion male workers. Adams and Joe Mahalick stole six hundred pounds of dynamite and stored it in a nearby cellar until the time was right to plant the bomb.

Apparently, Haywood got wind of their terrifying plan, intervened and flatly told them, "No."

Adams was secure in a jail cell in Ada County in 1907; his cell was located next to Haywood's, Moyer's and Pettibone's. The men never spoke to one another, as Adams refused.

The Murder of Sheriff Harvey K. Brown: October 10, 1907

Just weeks before his assault, Brown confessed, "I am a doomed man. Those people in Idaho will get me yet." Brown was a key witness in both the Adams/Tyler trial and the Steunenberg case.

Another bomb at the gate explosion (the same manner in which ex-governor Steunenberg was killed) rattled the life of ex-sheriff Harvey K. Brown of Wardner. He also encountered a fatal incident in which a bomb was attached the gate in front of his home that, when opened, tripped a wire and exploded. Brown's left leg was blown completely off and laid yards away in a mangled mesh of flesh and blood, and his right hip and leg were shattered. He knew he would not live. The telltall clue that the police would find the same killer involved was that both Steunenberg's gate and Brown's gate had two red crisscross chalk marks on them. Who made these markings? Was it Orchard and Adams or someone else marking the gates so that there would be no mess up with a bomb attached to someone else's gate? It remains a mystery.

Brown summoned District Attorney Leroy Lemax and his stenographer to his bedside to give a statement: "I was the man who arrested Steve Adams, which was instrumental in the capture of Harry Orchard. I knew too much about the connections of Steve Adams with the Western Federation of Miners, and it is the best interest to have him out of the way."

Adams claimed he had an alibi.

The following is Brown's antemortem statement (dying declaration):

> *I was on my way home from uptown last night when I met a man in front of a residence that is a block from my house and spoke. The man made no response. This man was about five feet, ten inches tall, weight was about 165 pounds. He wore a brown suit and a celluloid collar and was smoothly shaven. I have been conscious of having been followed for the past three weeks, and I have no doubt that those who attempted my life are persons connected with the Western Federation of Miners and that I was marked for death on account of my connection with the Steunenberg and Steve Adams case.*

Death Threats to Archie Phillips: Spring of 1908

Another man in connection with the Tyler murder was Archie Phillips. He was continually having his life threatened. Out of fear for his life, he soon fled Idaho and hid in the mountains for over a year in Canada. Phillips was the single lost witness in the case that would have made a huge difference. His testimony was the missing link that was so desperately needed for justice to be served and validate the connection between Adams and Tyler's murder.

He would have told the jury that the night before Tyler's killing, Steve Adams and J. Simpkins had stayed at Phillips's cabin in the woods. He would have told them that his wife did indeed kindly give all the men bottles of fresh horseradish. The horseradish was a link that connected the men together in the murder.

Before the second trial of Adams, Phillips began getting multiple death threats. Recently, two unknown men had visited Mrs. Phillips unannounced and told her sternly that her husband would be dead in one week if he did not leave the country. Since Phillips had a wife and two small children to care for, he decided it was best to leave town.

Just a few days later, as they promised, Phillips found a box of ten pounds of dynamite behind his house. Frightened for his family, he showed the evidence of foul play to Sheriff Brown (who would also be killed by a bomb explosion later), along with the letters he had received threatening his life.

Phillips, shaking, asked Sheriff Brown, "What are you going to do?"

Instead of addressing the crime, Sheriff Brown looked into Phillips's eyes and calmly said, "Increase my life insurance and stay home." And he walked away.

Phillips had no choice but to leave his family in the cabin in the woods and pray they would remain safe.

He quickly fled to Canada. The Pinkerton detectives and local police continued to search for him in vain.

Phillips told his friends, "If they [the Dynamite Band] get me, they get me."

The *Coeur d'Alene Evening Press* later wrote up Phillips's statement on April 3, 1908:

> *Would I testify against Adams now? The Idaho officials have made me no offers. I could get a good job now by going back, a place high in the state, but I'm not going back. No, Idaho is barred for me. Adams is in Colorado to answer for the Collins murder. I've got to live for my wife and the babies. I don't want to be mixed up in any case. I'm going to stay in the United States from now on. This is supposed to be the land of the common man. If I can't get protection from the officers, perhaps I can from the whole people.*

Eventually, Phillips did come back home to his wife and kids, thinking that since Adams never got convicted, the whole mess could be over with and the thugs would leave him alone.

Adams was tried two times in Idaho for the murder of Fred Tyler. The first time there was "no verdict," and the second time, he was acquitted. In

1907, the case was dismissed. He left the courtroom with William Easterly (a Federationist) and his wife, who loyally stood by his side the entire time, claiming his innocence. No other arrests were ever made, and no charges were ever brought forward for his other crimes. Adams was always a perfect gentleman and shook hands with every juror, whether they voted for his innocence or guilt.

The Assassination Attempt on General Wells: March 1908

Another man who was scheduled to testify against Adams was General Buckley Wells, the general manager of the Smuggler-Union Mine in Telluride, Colorado. On November 12, 1907, Wells testified in the Adams/Tyler trial. He told the jury that he had accompanied Adams to Colorado in order to assist in the location of a body that had been buried there. He did not disclose any more information on the matter. (Note: the murdered Arthur Collins was General Wells's predecessor.) If Adams was acquitted of the murder, he would go to Colorado to be tried for Collins's murder. Death threats had been thrust on General Wells, too. Early that spring, he had also received horrific letters stating that several mines in the area would be blown to smithereens if they did not get their way.

Wells was famous for a few things but mostly for digging up the bomb planted to kill Governor Peabody. He was also in charge of the special train that moved Moyer, Haywood and Pettibone from Denver to Boise, what would come to be known as the "Kidnapping Trip."

The Assassination Attempt of Governor Peabody and Judge Goddard

Harry Orchard and Steve Adams built a bomb to blow apart Governor James H. Peabody, the ex-governor of Colorado. Their first attempt was foiled because two coal wagons drove across the trip wires at the same time Peabody was crossing the road. Peabody had been receiving death threat letters ever since the Haywood trial began. He did not take them seriously, although he should have.

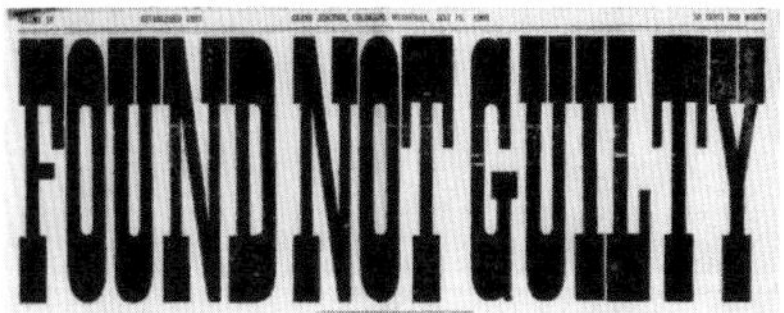
FOUND NOT GUILTY

Strangely, Steve Adams was found not guilty of the long list of terrible crimes he had committed and confessed to. *From the* Daily Sentinel, *July 15, 1908.*

Steve Adams and Harry Orchard were also watching Judge Goddard's house. The pretending-to-be-innocent Mrs. Adams would help divert the attention from the bombs, but at the last minute, Orchard chickened out, saying he was too cowardly to openly kill Judge Goddard.

Final Word on Adams

The final trial against Adams occurred on July 15, 1908. He was set free in Colorado with no other charges held against him. His old wealthy uncle William Lillard had footed a lot of the expense of his nephew's defense. He told the *Daily Sentinel*, "When any of my folks are in trouble and I think they are in the right, I am going to stand by them no matter what it costs." (It was reported he had spent almost $10,000 defending his nephew.) Steve Adams married Bertha McFadden on October 4, 1909, with just two witnesses at a very small and private ceremony. They moved to Harrison to build a life together. He had only been divorced from his first wife a short time.

The *Coeur d'Alene Evening Press* published a brief follow-up of Adams's life on October 20, 1909. Although the then-married Adams tried to lead a better life, after all was said and done, he got caught selling intoxicating liquors without a license and was again arrested.

A certificate of birth for their daughter, Laura Elizabeth, born on August 12, 1910, reveals that the forty-year-old Adams was working as a bartender in a saloon. He died in Spokane, Washington, on December 8, 1934, at the age of sixty-two.

Final Word on Orchard

Harry Orchard came to Spokane, Washington, in 1896. He then moved to Wallace, Idaho, where he worked driving a milk cart for the Markel Brothers. The next year, he moved to Burke and became involved in the Western Federation of Miners.

As Steve Adams's partner, he was equally guilty of many of the same horrific crimes throughout his lifetime that Adams was. Orchard, who was thought to have a psychotic personality disorder, confessed to murdering at least seventeen people, but there were probably more. He was also a bigamist and had left at least two wives to fend for themselves. He committed insurance fraud, derailed trains, blew up mines, stole livestock and stole from his employers.

Orchard pleaded guilty to the murder of Governor Steunenberg and was sentenced to death by hanging. His sentence was later reduced to life imprisonment. He ended up in the state penitentiary in Boise, Idaho, where he chose (and was allowed) to live the remainder of his years there in safety and peace (instead of being set free when the time came) at the taxpayers' expense, of course. He became religious and wrote his life's confessions in a published book. He was allowed to live in a small house outside of the prison and was in charge of tending to the prison's chickens and growing strawberries. He suffered a stroke in 1953 and became bedridden. Not long after that, he slipped into a coma. After almost fifty years in prison, he finally died at the age of eighty-eight on April 13, 1954. It was not a bad sentence or life, considering all the people he had murdered in cold blood.

1907: Murdered by a Best Friend

A bizarre twist between two best friends occurred late one night on April 25, 1907. The evening started out as a normal one, the streets filled with people drinking and enjoying the small town of Wallace.

But around 1:00 a.m., many lives were changed forever.

The two men (who were considered the best of friends) had a brief fight that ended with one man stone-cold dead.

That spring evening, Shoshone County jailer Carson C. Hicks was out for the night, strolling down Cedar Street in Wallace. He decided to stop in for a quick one at the Wallace Hotel. Sitting inside was his best friend, an ex-policeman named John William "Billy" Quinn. Both men were somewhat drunk.

When Quinn saw his friend enter the saloon, he smiled and raised his glass to Hicks.

"Here comes my Missouri friend, and we are going to have a drink together!"

But Hicks was in no mood for Quinn's banter. He quickly muttered back to Quinn, "Don't talk to me like that," and proceeded to say profanities under his breath.

No sooner did Quinn blink with shock, that his so-called best friend pulled out his revolver, aimed it straight at Quinn and pulled the trigger.

Quinn fell to the floor in a bloody heap. Three doctors, J.E. Jean, Mowery and Harris, were called in and tended to the dying man.

What were the men fighting about? What would have been so awful that Hicks would shoot Quinn in cold blood in front of witnesses?

No further information can be found about the murder, except that Hicks pleaded not guilty to the charge in May. Oddly, the local union for the Western Federation of Miners took an active interest in making sure Hicks got prosecuted for the crime. Even odder, Quinn's death certificate has absolutely nothing written in the "cause of death" section on the card. Why?

Quinn's body was shipped back to Portland, Oregon, for burial at the Riverview Cemetery. He was unmarried and left a grieving mother in Coeur d'Alene.

1907: Horton Kills Cramer in Osburn

Captain A.P. Horton and Mr. William Osburn owned a productive little saloon in downtown Osburn together. They kept the place tidy and its customers happy.

But in the fall of 1907, a local disorderly drunk named W.F. Cramer (also called Crazy Frenchy) stumbled his way into the saloon in the early hours on a Sunday morning. Captain Horton was still busy cleaning up from the night before and was in no mood for Crazy Frenchy's crap. He was obviously very intoxicated and needed no more to drink, so Captain Horton refused to serve him any more liquor. Besides, it was Sunday, and the new city rule, called the Sunday Rest Law, was in place, meaning alcohol could not be served.

Cramer was known in town to get mean and nasty when he was drunk. Everyone knew this. When Horton continued to refuse to serve the man, Cramer became furious and began smashing bar glasses on the floor, shattering them to bits and pieces. Horton demanded he stop his senseless tirade. This infuriated Cramer even more, and he quickly reached for his pistol, but the clear-minded Captain was quicker on the draw.

Threatened, he snatched his shotgun from under the bar, pointed it right at Cramer's reddened face and pulled the trigger. *Bang!* That was the end of Crazy Frenchy.

Animosity had been developing between the two men for years, and Crazy Frenchy had threatened to kill Captain Horton by poisoning him one too many times.

Horton calmly notified the sheriff of Wallace of what had happened and said that Frenchy was lying dead on the floor of his saloon. While he waited for the sheriff to arrive, Horton decided to stop cleaning and take the time to give himself a shave.

Frenchy was face-down in a pool of his own blood, his face then nothing more than a bloody pulp.

When Sheriff Bailey arrived, he questioned the six men who had also been in the bar at the time of the shooting, but they all said they didn't see much, as they were busy playing cards in the back room of the building.

Sheriff Bailey, Deputy Angus Sutherland and Chief of Police Victor Langley searched the dead man's coat and found the loaded revolver. Soon, Coroner D.E. Keyes arrived. His findings were not unusual for a victim who had just been shot in the face point-blank by a shot gun. His professional observation? Cramer suffered from a fractured jaw in five different places, causing instant death from a gunshot wound. No surprise there.

Captain Horton was a well-known and well-liked Coeur d'Alene pioneer. He came to the region in 1883, when he immediately became friends and partners with William Osburn.

Cramer was a Frenchmen and educated, but he had become a prolific drinker and had been in and out of jail multiple times. He was prospecting in the area at the time of his murder.

The jury agreed unanimously that Cramer's murder was a justifiable homicide.

Besides, no one really liked Crazy Frenchy anyway.

1908: UNSOLVED MURDERS OF NICHOLAS THORNTON AND GEORGE WEARING

An unsolved murder in Wallace, Idaho, was that of George Wearing (unknown–1903), a prominent gold miner from Telluride, Colorado, who was visiting the quaint small town for work. After a long day on June 4, 1903, he was participating in libations at a bar in town called the Royal Oak Saloon.

The series of events that fateful night that led to Wearing's demise were never revealed. He had not been in town long enough to acquire any real enemies, so was the motive robbery?

The coroner decided that Wearing had died from a fractured skull resulting from either a hard fall or a violent scuffle.

When the bartender (from the bar where Wearing was last seen drinking) was questioned about the man's death, he told the police that the patron had simply fallen down the stairs. Locals found this very suspicious, as his body was found on the floor inside the bowling alley at the Royal Oak. And besides, if the man had stumbled and fallen down the stairs, wouldn't the bartender or another patron have gone to assist him?

Wearing struggled to survive, but his injuries were too severe.

His family was summoned, and Wearing remained unconscious until his death. There was only one sliver of a moment when he opened his eyes to this world for the final time. His crying son was standing next to him. As soon as his father's eyes fluttered open, his son demanded, "Who did this to you, Dad?" But the question went unanswered. His father died right before his eyes without so much as a peep as to who had assaulted him.

George Wearing took one final breath and moved out of this world and into the next.

No further information or follow-up investigation can be found, and Wearing's ruthless murder remains unsolved to this day.

Another unsolved Wallace murder under eerily similar and mysterious circumstances (just a few years after Wearing's death) was that of a man known as Nicholas Thornton (1838–1908).

Friendly drinking in Wallace, Idaho, has been prominent since the day the town was established, but not always does it end on a good note. Such was the case in 1908 when seventy-year-old Nicolas Thornton, a former Wallace pioneer, decided to toss back a few shots of whiskey one cold night.

On December 30, Thornton was walking the streets of Wallace and loitering in and out of the bars, enjoying some libations and chatting with the locals. He seemed to be in good spirits, and nothing seemed out of the ordinary.

But later that night, under strange circumstances, Thornton's dead body was found in the alley near the Wallace Hotel on Cedar Street.

Somewhere along the line in Thornton's nights of carousing, he had encountered fatal trouble.

His untimely death was a mystery. All anyone knew about the crime was that he had died very early on that Monday morning, after a hard night of drinking in Wallace.

As Thornton lay dead in the alley, no one could figure out what had happened to him that could have caused his demise. Since there was no blood at the scene, it was agreed that he probably had just died from natural causes (a stroke or heart attack), and the matter was left at that.

Soon, grieving friends and family members were preparing the Eagles Hall in town for Thornton's funeral. Men slowly began moving his body from the undertakers over to the Eagles Hall for the memorial.

The Wallace Corner Hotel in Wallace today. Several unsolved murders occurred in this location in the early 1900s. *Author's collection.*

But when Coroners Dr. Hugh France and Dr. F.L. Quigly reviewed their facts and findings, they came to a startling conclusion. They both discovered some very disturbing evidence during their autopsies.

Thornton did not die of a stroke or heart attack as assumed; instead, he suffered a severe fracture to his skull that caused a huge blood clot to form in his brain, killing him instantly. They both felt the fatal injury was the direct result of the man being bludgeoned and forcibly thrown down into the street from the Wallace Hotel's bar—the same coroner's conclusion in Wearing's murder.

Much to the surprised mourner's dismay, the coroners hurriedly stopped the funeral and revealed that they immediately needed to notify the police of a possible homicide.

So while the victim's body was still lying in the coffin at the Eagles Hall, the mourners were asked to leave, and a coroner's inquest was started without delay. The inquest dragged on and on until 11:15 p.m., and with no conclusive results, it was adjourned until the following day.

Police needed to find the only material witness to the crime, a man known simply as Dorth, for questioning. But mysteriously, Dorth had quickly been sent out of town by a stranger, so he could not testify to the affair and could not be tracked down.

The jury did not agree to the fact that Thornton's death was caused by violent means. It was unclear to them if Thornton's death was just a tragic accident or an actual homicide.

Mr. Nicolas Thornton was buried in the Eagle section at Nine Mile Cemetery in Wallace. No further information or follow-up investigation can be found, and Thornton's murder remains unsolved to this day.

His body rests at the Nine Mile Cemetery in Wallace in the Eagles section, row 7.

1915: Wrong Place, Wrong Time

A man named W.H. "Doc" Cain met a terrible end, as a stranger to him, Patrick (also known as Daniel Taylor and Henry Kenedy) Murphy, shot and killed Doc during a robbery.

Doc was in the Depot Saloon in Kellogg, Idaho, on the night of August 18, 1915, enjoying a few libations with his friends. No sooner had the men finished their whiskey than a stranger barged into the saloon and demanded the bartender hand over the money in the drawer or be shot. The bartender, fearing for his life, handed over the enormous sum of $500 to the bandit.

As most men in the bar froze in fear, poor Doc Cain tried to stop the robber as he exited the bar. Unfortunately, that would be the last honorable thing Doc would do. Murphy shot him dead on the spot.

Murphy was no stranger to violence and drunken debauchery. Earlier that month, while drinking heavily in the nearby town of Wallace, Murphy

Killer Patrick Murphy shot an innocent victim, Doc Cain, as he robbed a saloon in Kellogg in 1915. *Courtesy of the Idaho State Penitentiary and Ancestry.*

became intoxicated and was told by police to either go to jail or leave town. Murphy said he chose to leave town.

But he didn't leave town. He stayed.

Soon, he was arrested a second time for the same reason, being drunk and disorderly. This time, the judge ordered ten days of hard labor as his punishment. Murphy, who should have left town, found himself working in the awful field for the local sewerage department. He certainly should have left town. Before his ten days were up, he begged to be let go. He was relieved and was told a third time to leave the area. But just two days after his warning, Murphy was still in the area and back to drinking and acting like an idiot. Some people never learn.

After the murder of Doc Cain, locals blamed the judge for Cain's untimely murder. If Murphy had completed his ten days of hard labor, would he have killed Cain? The reality of it was that Murphy would have gotten into some sort of trouble, regardless of whether he was released early or not. He may not have robbed the exact saloon that cost Cain his life, but he would have done something else just as bad.

Doc Cain was a watchman employed at the Bunker Hill and Sullivan Mine in Kellogg. He was a hardworking and well-liked man in town and never got into trouble. He was just in the wrong place at the wrong time. After the trial, Murphy pled guilty to first-degree murder, and on September 9, Judge Woods in Wallace sentenced him to life in prison. Murphy's real name was Daniel W. Taylor, and he was born in Texas.

Cain Reunited with His Past

Curiously, a woman who lived at 1613 Grand Avenue in Spokane named Georgia Richardson noticed the victim's name in the paper and wondered if it was the same man her mother had been married to twenty years prior. She had not stayed in touch with her stepfather, as she was just a baby the last time she saw Cain. He had lived in Moscow, Idaho, for twenty years and later moved to Coeur d'Alene. Excited, Georgia mailed her only photograph of her stepfather to her friends in Wallace to see if it was the same man who had gotten killed.

They verified the dead man's identity to Georgie. It was indeed her former stepfather.

Miss Georgia Richardson was able to attend her stepfather's funeral in Kellogg. She was able to say one final goodbye to the man she once knew and loved as her stepfather in 1895.

1916: Herman Rossi Kills Guitarist in Jealous Rage

One of the most sensationalized trials of north Idaho was the court case that involved the ex-mayor of Wallace, Idaho, named Herman J. Rossi (1870–1937), who shot his wife's lover in cold blood in front of multiple witnesses—and was let go with barely a warning.

It was a cold afternoon in October 1916 when Rossi was finally coming home from a business trip in Boise, Idaho. Upon his arrival, he first went to his office to take care of an urgent business matter before heading to his house at 221 Cedar Street in Wallace.

When he arrived unannounced that evening, he was in for a big surprise.

His young wife, Mabel, was disheveled, drunk and unconscious in the bed. Rossi looked around the room, which was an utter mess. He also noticed their bedframe was then bent for some odd reason he could only imagine. His wife had a few dark bruises about her person. He roused his wife out of her stupor and demanded to know what had been going on while he was gone. She admitted that Dahlquist had supplied her with alcohol and that they had spent two nights and a day together in the Rossi home (and in bed). Mabel casually assured her husband that if she *did* have sex with her friend, it was only because she was drunk.

Rossi became wild with a jealous rage.

He stormed downstairs and confronted their housekeeper, Ruth Melville, inquiring about what exactly had been going on in his house in his absence. She quietly told him that a man named Gabe had been hanging out there, partying with Mabel for the last few days (and nights).

The bungalow Herman Rossi built in Wallace for his philandering wife, Mabel. Here, she entertained her lover while he was in Boise working. *Author's collection.*

Rossi marched back up the stairs, grabbed Mabel, and they began to fight. Mabel was able to break free from Rossi and locked herself behind the safety of a door.

In an attempt to calm Rossi, Ruth poured him a cup of coffee.

But Rossi was fuming. He took out his anger on his poor housekeeper.

After a few minutes, he got up, grabbed his coat and headed out the door. He grabbed again at the maid in anger. She quickly pulled away.

Ruth called to him, "Where are you going?" But he ignored her.

The front door slammed behind Rossi as he went out into the streets of Wallace.

His life would never be the same. In the next few minutes, his rage would get the best of him, and the rest would make legal history.

A few blocks away, Clarence "Gabe" Dahlquist was calmly drinking in the lobby at the Samuels Hotel with some friends. Rossi burst through the door in a huff and immediately found Dahlquist. He was sitting in a chair with his back to Rossi. Rossi marched toward his wife's lover and beat him over the head a few times with his .38-caliber revolver. Dahlquist jumped up and started to run away from his assailant. As he was running, Rossi pointed the gun at him and fired a single shot. Dahlquist plunged to the

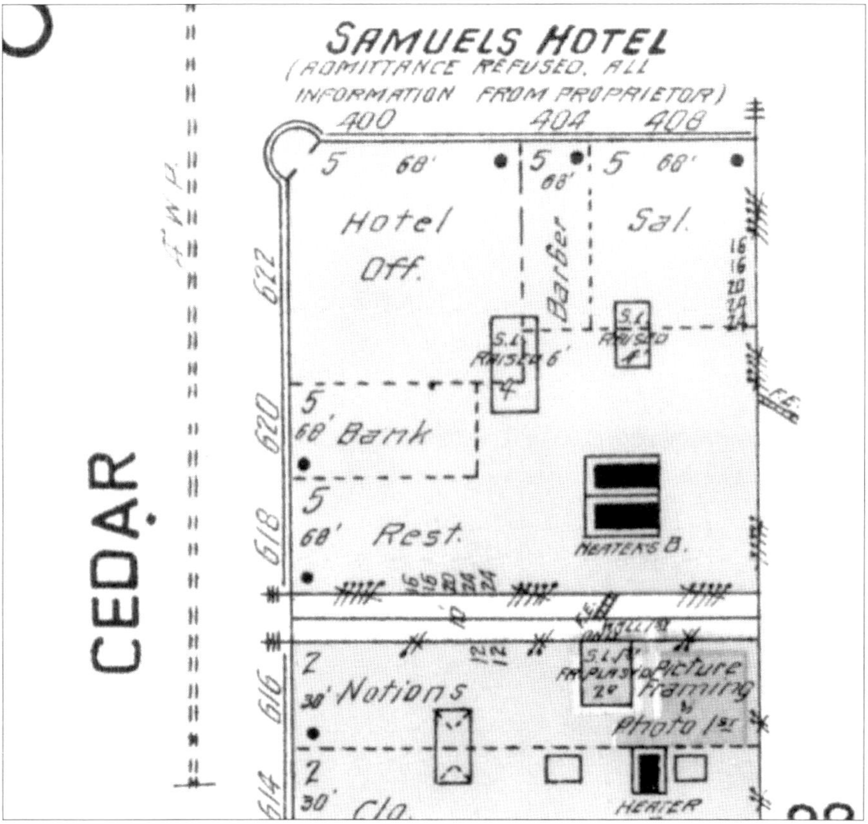

A Sandborn map from 1908, which indicates that "admittance was refused" by the proprietor. It does give a general layout of the lobby. *Courtesy of the Library of Congress.*

floor and hid behind some furniture. Panicked and scared to death, he had been shot in the lung.

Rossi wanted to shoot his wife's lover a second time just for good measure, but he was interrupted by the hotel clerk George Baxter and another employee named Mrs. Laura Stone, who both warned him to stop. At one point, Baxter yelled to Rossi, "For God's sake, Herman, don't shoot!"

Rossi seemed to come out of his rage and returned to his normal state of mind. He waved his gun around and demanded Dahlquist to "Leave town or else!"

Dahlquist agreed he would promptly leave town.

But Dahlquist was in no shape to leave Wallace. (Instead, he would soon be fighting for his life in a bed at the hospital.)

The only remaining piece of Samuels' Hotel in Wallace is the tiled entry. The hotel's former location is now a city park. *Author's collection.*

The grand Samuel's Hotel was considered the finest hotel in the Silver Valley. *From the Barnard-Stockbridge Photograph Collection, Digital Initiatives, University of Idaho Library, public domain.*

The old office (*marked with an arrow*) of Herman Rossi when he worked as an insurance broker in Wallace. *Author's collection.*

The flustered Rossi left Samuels Hotel, went back out into the crisp air and began walking down the street. Soon, he ran into two buddies, Walter Hanson and Julius Goodrich. They asked him what he was up to, and Rossi muttered something under his breath. The men parted ways. Within seconds, the men heard of the shooting and hurriedly went to Rossi's office, where the found him alone, frazzled and contemplating his recent actions.

When they confronted Rossi about shooting Dahlquist, he simply said, "If I shot him, I don't know it, and I am sorry." They carefully extracted the gun from him and took Rossi back to Hanson's office, where (after calming Rossi down) he was given up to policeman James Collins. A hefty $10,000 bail was quickly placed, of which Rossi's good friends and associates ponied up the money for him, and he was released that very same night.

On the other side of town, Dahlquist's body could not take the strain of the gunshot wound, and he died at 3:00 p.m. the next day. This forced the officers to rearrest Rossi now for "deliberate and premeditated" murder.

The worn-out Rossi, who probably hadn't gotten a wink of sleep all night, was then facing an incredible $50,000 bail. (This would be about a whopping $1,264,437 today.)

Worry must have coursed through Rossi's veins once he heard of the bail amount incurred against his release. But low and behold, his very good friends Eugene R. Day, James F. McCarthy, Henry White, George Steward, M.J. Flohr, H.E. Howes, O.A. Olin, W.A. Simons, L.L. Sweet and John Lucas all pooled their money together and tried to get Rossi released.

An illustration of Mabel Rossi, the wife of Herman Rossi. Her infidelity was the reason Herman killed her lover, Gabe Dahlquist. *From the* Tacoma Times, *1916.*

Back at the Rossi house, Mabel quickly packed her things, left town and was not heard from for some time.

The funeral procession for Dahlquist was spectacular. His casket was drawn by two elegant horses in a fine carriage. The crowd was overwhelming. Obviously, Dahlquist was a well-loved person and talented musician in Wallace. After the procession, his buddies and fellow Elk Lodge members got his casket loaded properly into the railroad car in town at the Northern Pacific Depot, and his body was soon carted off back to Nebraska, where his family resided and where he would be laid to rest.

At the courthouse, Rossi's defense attorney, Walter Hanson, waived his right to a preliminary trial. (The fact that Rossi shot Dahlquist in front of many witnesses really could not be disputed.) Rossi's attorney was hoping to avoid the risk of a change of venue submitted by the prosecuting attorney. If Rossi was going to "get off" on the charge of murder, it would need to be with the local support of his hometown buddies. Judge Weniger was not in a giving mood this fine day, and he refused Rossi being released on the whopping $50,000 dollar bail.

During the trial, Rossi pleaded, "I do not know the whereabouts of my wife," as he suppressed a sob. "The home I gave her was good. It had satisfied my first wife. But to give her [Mabel] a home that would be more in accord

The beautiful courthouse in Wallace where many criminals were put behind bars in the 1900s. Today, it houses government offices. *Author's collection.*

with her ideas, I built her a new one, a two-story concrete bungalow that cost me $13,000 [$313,686 today] to build the house alone. I furnished it nicely, and my wife was never without servants."

It was also noted that he had spent the last decade trying to get Mabel sober and free from the clutch of alcohol.

Rossi was handcuffed and escorted to the jail in town, which was then in the basement of the Shoshone County Courthouse in Wallace.

The trial was an extensive one, with much interest throughout Idaho, since Rossi was a huge player in several areas, including the town of Wallace, Shoshone County and the state of Idaho. The lawyers went back and forth.

The defense demanded that Rossi was in such a state of rage and jealousy that his emotions were causing him to be temporarily insane.

Prosecution laughed and argued that insane or not, Rossi had murdered Dahlquist in cold blood without justification or self-defense.

After much ado and back-and-forth arguing, charges of temporary insanity and a long, tiresome trial, the jury finally came to a verdict. It seems as though everyone was sympathetic to Rossi's predicament.

An old Rossi insurance advertisement that was placed in the *Wallace Miner* in August 31, 1916.

Rossi was unanimously acquitted of the murder. The courtroom cheered with screams of joy. Rossi, worn and extremely exhausted from the whole mess, shook the hands of each jury member, thanking them for their vote to free him.

The morning headlines read: "Unwritten Law Frees Rossi from Murder Charges!"

Rossi was released. Some suggested that the pair would reconcile, but that was only a rumor. Rossi's lawyer reassured the townsfolk that Herman Rossi was 100 percent through with that woman.

Mabel and Rossi continued to battle it out in the courts over property and money, but they were eventually divorced. Mabel left town, and her future whereabouts are unknown.

Rossi started courting (and soon married) another woman named Mabel, but that is another story entirely.

3

COEUR D'ALENE TRAGEDIES

Nightlife is filled with personal tragedies.
—Naguib Mahfouz

Northern Idaho has its share of strange tragedies and unsolved mysteries. Some tell of a secret underwater naval training submarine station that is hidden deep within the muddy water of Lake Pend Oreille north of Coeur d'Alene (which is true). Others claim there is a mysterious Loch Ness of Idaho slinking through the same waters (which is unknown). Tales of sunken ships, horse skeletons and bodies of murdered men also circulate.

Other legends are more probable, like that of the robbery in Wallace that occurred in 1900. A local bank was robbed, and the bandits made off with an incredible $80,000. Knowing they were being pursued by a posse, they quickly buried the loot somewhere between Huettner and Post Falls. The posse met up with the bank robbers, who were promptly hanged on the spot, the $80,000 never to be found. The over-eager sheriff should have waited to hang the men until they at least confessed as to where they hid the money. To this day, the treasure has never been found. Will some lucky person be gardening someday and stumble upon a small fortune while planting petunias?

Another tale involves the famous outlaw Butch Cassidy and his gang. The bandits were carrying a large sum of stolen money, and marshals were hot on their trail. They hastily buried their stolen goods and money on an

The *Idaho* steamer was similar to the one that collided with a group of logs that killed five people in 1887. One man who died was carrying over $10,000 worth of cash in his suitcase. *From the* Coeur d'Alene Press, *August 29, 1907.*

old stagecoach road somewhere between Spokane Falls and Wallace. The only clue recorded was that they hid the loot along a creek between a rock and a beaver dam.

Northern Idaho has seen its fair share of bizarre mysteries and awful tragedies over the years.

1887: SINKING STEAMER KILLS PASSENGERS

A horrible Lake Coeur d'Alene tragedy involving a steamer called *Spokane*, owned and operated by Captain Nelson Martin, occurred in 1887 and took five lives. The local steamer left Kingston, Idaho, on April 4 and headed up the river.

Unfortunately, Martin was an inexperienced boat man, as most of his previous employment was driving a stagecoach for his business, Spokane Falls and Coeur d'Alene Stage Line. This was also his first voyage running the *Spokane* on the unpredictable Coeur d'Alene River.

The twenty-five-foot-long steamer began moving out of control, and soon its hull hit a massive group of logs. It completely rolled over on its side and capsized when it was caught up in a strong current. All twenty-four passengers were sunk, but most managed to swim to shore. The victims who drowned were J.C. Hanna, Lorenzo Pike, Ed Jerome, Colonel N.J. Higgins and one unknown deckhand.

Although Higgins's dead body was recovered, it was soon discovered that his trunk had over $60,000 in cash in it. Where did all that money come from? Where was Higgins going with his trunk full of cash? Where did the $60,000 eventually go? No records can be found.

An unidentified eyewitness told his version of what happened to the *Lewiston Teller* on April 16:

> *The river divided into two parts, with an island of driftwood in the middle. We hit the logs, and the moment she touched the log, I jumped off with three companions and landed safely. The boat swung off and in another moment struck a log below and capsized, pitching all on board into the middle of the river. Pike caught onto a log a short distance away and hung on for some time but let go and sank from sight.…I saw Mr. Hanna come up once and thought he had caught onto the boat. Mr. Higgins never came to the surface, not a word was spoken and I did not hear a man cry out. We had nothing to work with, and it was impossible to render any assistance. I had a revolver and loaded and fired it a number of times, which attracted the people of Kingston, and a number of boats arrived and rendered all the aid in their power. It was a horrible spectacle, especially since myself and companions were unable to render the struggling people any assistance. The survivors are now all right.*

Deputy United States marshal Greene went fifty feet under the strong tow and was stuck in a large pile of wood, where he was slightly strangled but was later saved. A man named Charles Wood was able to get unlodged from the logs and taken to safety.

The captain and the engineer were arrested for the accident.

1889: 150 Tons of Ore at the Bottom of Lake Coeur d'Alene

Coeur d'Alene Lake was busy with lots of steamships that were being used to transport people, mining and lumber mill equipment and various supplies during the late 1800s and early 1900s. Coeur d'Alene was a popular railroad and steamboat transfer point and hub for goods being delivered between the mines and the nearby smelters. The prominent Spokane businessman, D.C.

Corbin, decided to cash in on this activity and turned two steamers into ore carriers for on the Lake Coeur d'Alene.

In the late fall of 1889, Captain Nisbet was in charge of towing two heavily loaded steamboats down the lake from the Old Mission area with the ice-breaking *Kootenai*. Each steamship in tow carried over 150 tons of silver ore. As Captain Nisbet slowly and carefully worked his way down the partially frozen river, he soon realized he was in trouble. The loads were becoming unstable. To avoid losing one of the carriers, he made his way toward the shoreline and had his crew remove and tie one of them off at the bank to be retrieved later.

Around midnight, the captain and his crew decided the worst of it was over; they were out of harm's way, and the exhausted team could get some much-needed sleep.

But they wouldn't sleep long. Soon, fireman Fred Wilson noticed the barge was tipping over to one side. Hurriedly, he notified the captain of the problem. The crew was awoken, bells were rung, the engine was cut to half speed and the team was put to work immediately trying to level the barge.

The captain soon called out, "Let's try to make it to shore!" They were located about a half mile from McDonald's Point.

When they almost got to shore, the barge faltered. The burlap bags of ore had been loaded in three long rows, rising over four feet in height. The frustrated crew watched in astonishment as one row slowly dropped into the river. The weight of the boat faltered, and soon, the other side was dipping toward the water, and another row of ore went into the depths below. As the weight change again made the barge rock from side to side, most of the middle pile of ore also made its way into the lake.

Within seconds, over 150 tons of silver ore sank to the bottom of Lake Coeur d'Alene, taking with it the $15,000 of profit that slowly sunk to the bottom, never to be retrieved.

Once notified of the disaster, the Northern Pacific Railroad brought in a diver to access the situation. The divers discovered that the ore was between sixty and one hundred feet below the icy surface. The cost of recovery would be more than what the ore was worth, so they left it.

A few have tried to retrieve the ore but have failed.

If an ambitious person with the right equipment could retrieve the ore and gather the 135,000 ounces of silver today, they would be $3,289,000 richer.

Anyone interested in taking a dive?

1907: Metcalf Shoots Himself in the Heart

Suicide is one of the most shocking tragedies of them all.

At 6:00 a.m. on May 27, 1907, the loud shot from a Winchester rifle rang through the air, waking the neighbors. As they roused from their slumbers, wondering what the commotion was all about, they had no idea that just blocks away, a man lay dead in a pool of his own blood.

John Metcalf, who lived on North Fourth Street in Coeur d'Alene, decided to end his life by shooting himself through his heart.

Sadly, he had threatened to kill himself before, and no one took him seriously.

This particular morning, Mrs. Metcalf was downstairs cooking breakfast for her husband. As the smell of bacon and coffee permeated the house, her life would soon take a turn for the worst.

Mr. Metcalf was upstairs sitting on their bed with a .38-55 Winchester rifle, the muzzle pointed at his chest. He had been contemplating pulling the trigger for several minutes.

And then he went for it.

The loud *boom* of the rifle's shot rang through the house, waking the family's eight hungry children.

Mrs. Metcalf quickly ran upstairs, fearing the worst. When she opened the door to their bedroom, she found her husband sitting in a pool of blood. Surprisingly, he was still alive.

She quickly summoned Dr. Wood, who ran over and examined her husband. The wound was extensive, and Dr. Wood did not have to verbalize what Mrs. Metcalf already knew. Mr. Metcalf's death quickly followed. The shocked widow was inconsolable. What was she going to do?

As his body was taken to Coeur d'Alene Undertaking, the neighbors eagerly jumped in to help the poor woman and her traumatized children.

It was soon discovered that the Metcalf family was in dire need of help; the children were all under fed and malnourished.

After this tragedy, the citizens banded together and provided for Mrs. Metcalf and her children.

That is what the good people of Coeur d'Alene did—they helped those in times of need.

1909: MISSING TEENAGER FEIGNS SUICIDE

When the son of the wealthy Dr. Fulkerson mysteriously went missing, the city of Coeur d'Alene became frantic. On April 27, 1909, Raymond, just seventeen years old, simply vanished into thin air. He disappeared Sunday on his way to attend Sunday school. He did not return home that evening, something the boy would never do. When morning arrived and Raymond still hadn't shown up at the house, they knew something was terribly wrong. His parents feared the worst.

The prominent Dr. E.R. Fulkerson and his wife were incredibly distraught. The only evidence of what had happened to Raymond was a suicide letter supposedly written by the boy.

Why would he want to kill himself? There was no plausible reason. Was it a kidnapping? Was he going to be held for ransom? Did he truly commit suicide? There were so many questions left unanswered.

They received a handwritten letter on Monday that was postmarked Sunday from their son, oddly describing the scene that was something like this:

> *Dear Mom and Dad,*
>
> *When you receive this letter, I will be no more. My clothes and the revolver I have taken from my father's bureau could be found on the lake shore on the east end of the lake south of the Coeur d'Alene Lumber Company Mill. My body would be found in the lake.*
>
> *Your son, Ray*

The frightened parents set out immediately to search for Ray, following the directions he had disclosed in the letter, but they were not able to find anything or their son.

Frantic, they returned to town and contacted Reverend Fry, telling them of the urgent matter. Worried, Reverend Fry began to gather his coat and hat to go search for the boy himself.

Just as he was leaving the church, Chief of Police McGovern approached him.

McGovern told the reverend that he and some locals had been searching for Ray all morning.

A man named W.L. Miles found the boy's clothing and his father's gun on a rock near the water's edge of Lake Coeur d'Alene approximately five hundred feet from the Coeur d'Alene Lumber Mill and just five feet from the water.

Although the boy's suit, necktie and collar and shirt were found, curiously, his hat and shoes were missing.

When McGovern checked the gun's chambers, a single bullet was discharged. Yet if it was a suicide by shooting, why was there no blood at the scene?

The possibility of suicide by drowning entered the inspector's thoughts. Did the boy chicken out when he held the gun to his head and instead walk out into the lake to die by suicide? Then why did he discharge the gun? Did he simply miss as he pulled the gun away from his head? Had he shot the gun at a nearby attacker?

McGovern walked down to the water to see if he could find any more clues. He noticed that it would be fairly impossible to drown in the area where the clothing articles and gun were found, as the lake was littered with many huge boulders for quite a way out. Any one of these rocks would give a person a place to safely stand. Did the boy know how to swim?

There was one other thing the inspector realized: the wind was terrible during this time and moving in the direction of the shore. If Ray had drowned, his body would have been swept in toward the large rocks, not moved outward in the lake.

When the reverend and inspector went back to Ray's parents to tell them of the discovery of their son's clothing and the father's gun, they were told of a possible motive for the suicide. They learned that their son was in love with an unknown female student at Spokane High School while he was also a student there (the girl apparently did not reciprocate his feelings). They showed the inspector the suicide note they had received that very morning. They also noted that his extra suit was missing from his trunk.

A team was assembled to drag the lake between the Coeur d'Alene Lumber Mill and the point at Tubb's Hill for Ray's body. None was ever found.

Three days went by without any sign of Ray or his body. His father, upon searching the boy's room, stumbled across a diary of sorts. Inside, the boy had written a few possible clues in his disappearance. Inside the book, he read, "Thirteen miles to Hauser."

The book also contained a list of multiple names.

Early May brought unexpected news to Raymond's worried parents. A letter arrived that advised them that Raymond was alive and well living in Lincoln, Nebraska, the former town of the Fulkerton family.

In Lincoln, Ray was well known and liked and found a job right away. Apparently, he missed his hometown and decided to return to it. But why would he pretend to commit suicide? Why would he put his family through so much turmoil?

The faux suicide of Raymond Fulkerton will never be explained.

4
PROHIBITION AND PROSTITUTION

Prohibition in Coeur d'Alene and the Silver Valley

To alcohol! The cause of...and solution to...all of life's problems!
—*Matt Groening*

Before Prohibition, more alcohol was consumed in Idaho than in any other state. Although Coeur d'Alene went "dry" in 1909, it did little to stop people from indulging in intoxicating beverages. By 1913, people were consuming the most liquor, tobacco, cigars, cigarettes and beer in the nation's history. The *Daily Star Mirror* announced on July 3, 1913, that there had been 143,300,000 gallons of whiskey produced and 64,500,000 barrels of beer (the numbers were probably exaggerated). They also claimed they collected $344,426,884 in liquor taxes.

In 1919 the Eighteenth Amendment of the Constitution was changed to "prohibit the manufacturing and sale of intoxicating liquors." Then in October the same year, Congress passed the Volstead Act that allowed the law to actually be enforced, so the demand for Prohibition agents was at an all-time high. Prohibition finally came to a well-received end in 1933.

One of the more popular saloons and brothels in Coeur d'Alene was named the Little Brick. It was owned by the notorious Fatty Carroll. This "hussie house" kept the local men happy and the local sheriff busy with arrests.

Above: An unknown man shows a sample of the whiskey from a moonshine still that had recently been confiscated by the Internal Revenue Bureau. It was photographed at the Treasury Department in 1921 during Prohibition. *Courtesy of the Library of Congress, no. 89706121.*

Left: Deputy Sheriff Adams was a very active and well-liked policeman in the Silver Valley. *From the* Rathdrum Tribune, *July 31, 1908.*

The never-ending career of bootlegging moonshine kept Coeur d'Alene's Sheriff Bailey and his assistants, D.R. Adams and Sawyer very busy. Judge Dunn was never bored either. Daily raids of saloons and dance halls were ordered in the city to try to maintain order. If a bar owner was found to be serving alcohol, they would incur a $300 fine and earn three months in jail.

In northern Idaho in the 1920s, many would come to violate the National Prohibition Act, and soon, the bail jumped up to $2,000 per incident, which would be paid by the saloon owners to the local sheriff.

This business of bootlegging was frowned on and taken very seriously. During this time, the production and selling of alcohol was a felony, and distillers and traffickers could be shot and killed on the spot.

Fortunately, most officers and officials drank, too, so they were a little more merciful.

Handmade whiskey stills were cropping up in hidden spots all over the town. They were hidden in barns, the woods, basements, attics, anywhere they could be set up. These men who took to manufacturing alcohol illegally were called moonshiners. And they became experts at being discreet. The policemen had to search for stills on foot, since they were most often tucked away from obvious places.

The moonshiners were a crafty bunch, though. They developed a cunning way to trick the cops to avoid being captured or followed. They carved fake cow hooves out of wood and attached them to their shoes. This way, the police would not be able to track them, as the tracks looked just like any other cow hoofprint. Some say the cow shoes idea spring from a Sherlock Holmes story in which the bad guy made horseshoes for his steed that looked like a cow's hoof, not a traditional horseshoe.

Men were not the only ones being sneaky during Prohibition. Women also got in on the action. They developed ways to hide a flask without obvious detection. Tiny flasks could be snuck into a boot or a cane. They could even be hidden discreetly beneath a woman's lacey garter.

When a raid was successful, the officers promptly poured the barrels of alcohol down the sewer drains, much to the dismay of thirsty onlookers.

A handsome and rugged hero whom the local press called "Two Gun Hart" and the "Beau of the Coeur d'Alenes" was actually the secret brother of the notorious Chicago gang leader Al "Scarface" Capone. The brothers ran on opposite sides of the law, and Two Gun Hart (whose real name was James Vincenzo Capone, but local people knew him as Richard J. Hart) felt it would be best if he hid his true identity from the world. Throughout

Opposite: During Prohibition, people had to get innovative when hiding their booze. In this image, an unidentified woman is concealing her whiskey in a flask inside her boot. *Courtesy of the Library of Congress, no.* 89714357.

This page, top: (*Right to left*) Lieutenant O.T. Davis, Sergeant J.D. McQuade, George Fowler of the Internal Revenue Service and H.G. Bauer with the largest illegal still ever retrieved in 1922. *Courtesy of the Library of Congress, no. 91796643.*

This page, bottom: Prohibition "cow shoes" in 1924, which were used when hiding their whiskey stills from police. The officers would often search for men's shoe tracks to lead them to the stills. *Courtesy of the Library of Congress, no. 2016849213.*

During Prohibition, the latest trend in flasks were "garter" flasks. In this image, dancer Mademoiselle Rhea shows off her flask as well as her legs. *Courtesy of the Library of Congress, no. 90709355.*

In 1921, as horrified onlookers watched, Deputy Police Commissioner John Leach (*right*) oversaw agents pouring a barrel of illegal liquor into the sewer following a raid during Prohibition. *Courtesy of the Library of Congress, no. 99405169.*

his career as a Prohibition agent, he arrested hundreds of bootleggers and moonshiners. Hart was adventurous and rugged and would travel via horseback (on his horse named Buckskin Betty), automobile, snowshoes or skis—whatever it took to pursue and catch his criminal. His record tallied the capture of over twenty murderers and countless arrests. He became a legendary hero to local citizens and a much-hated predicament to bootleggers and moonshiners. He would dress in various costumes to portray the image of a common working man or drunk in order to get leads on who was making and selling illegal booze.

Hart stayed as far away from his criminal brother as possible. By the 1920s, Al "Scarface" had become a multimillionaire by operating brothels, gambling halls and running illegal booze. He also made his millions by using bribery, murder and torture, things that the older white sheep Capone could live without. Headline after headline appeared, with the famous Al Capone being written up for one crime after another. Hart turned a blind eye to his notorious brother's violent criminal behavior and just lived his own life.

Near the end of their lives, they repaired their brotherly love.

The notorious gangster Al Capone had a baby brother named Two-Gun Hart who obeyed the laws in Idaho. *From Wikimedia, public domain, Alcatraz inmates.*

Why did Prohibition finally come to an end? Strangely, it was because of a mass shooting by Al Capone's gang in Chicago. On February 14, 1929, several men (some disguised as police officers) began shooting their machine guns at seven men in a garage. Over two thousand bullets were fired within seconds. All seven men were instantly dead, each corpse housing thirty or more bullets. Al Capone was a big-time enemy of his rival bootlegging Irish gang leader, George "Bugs" Moran. Capone wanted complete control over the bootlegging in Chicago.

This was the straw that broke the camel's back for Prohibition America. The thirteen-year Prohibition run had been a complete failure on many levels. Physicians were prescribing whiskey to their patients. Stills were built everywhere. People were still drinking. Local crime went through the roof. Organized crime had certainly flourished, and the illegal sale of alcohol was making the drug lords millions, while sadly, federal tax dollars dwindled. The law just didn't make sense anymore, so it was repealed.

President Franklin D. Roosevelt issued a proclamation declaring the end of Prohibition and asked the country to drink responsibly. He told the public, "I trust in the good sense of the American people." The president said "that they will not bring upon themselves the curse of excessive use of intoxicating liquors to the detriment of health, morals and social integrity."

Well, the decision was a good one for the federal government, as it collected $258 million in alcohol taxes in just one year.

PROSTITUTION COMES TO A HALT IN THE SILVER VALLEY

I believe that sex is one of the most beautiful, natural, wholesome things that money can buy.
—Steve Martin

A whopping four hundred–plus prostitutes worked in the Coeur d'Alene region between 1880 and 1911 to keep the miners and logging men happy. This "necessary evil" was tolerated due to the fact that many citizens felt the service provided kept countless girls and women safe from unruly men. The ratio of men to women during these years was very unbalanced.

In the years between 1878 and 1898, Coeur d'Alene was a military town with thousands of soldiers stationed at Fort Sherman. These men would be eager to spend their paychecks, and come pay day, they would travel to the city to partake in gambling, whoring and drinking.

The historic Lux rooms in Wallace that used to be an active bordello. It closed in the late 1980s. Today, they offer boutique-style hotel rooms above the wonderful Silver Corner Bar. *Author's collection.*

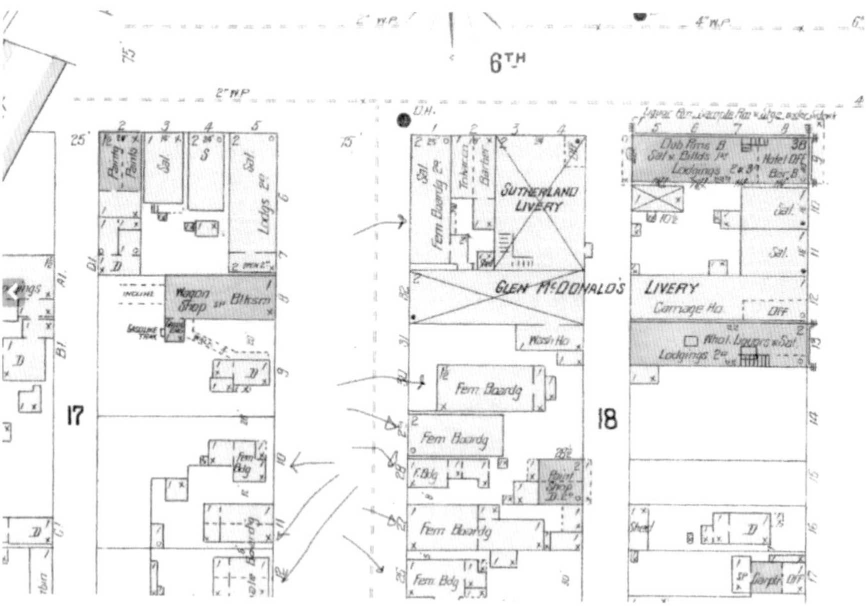

This Sanborn map from 1901 shows the extent of "female boardinghouses" in Wallace (marked with arrows). These were brothels, cribs and other buildings used for prostitution. *Courtesy of the Library of Congress.*

Unfortunately, the women would often rob the men while they were sleeping. Some men were even killed over a few bucks. If the men did not return to the barracks, it was assumed they ran off. Unless someone complained, no search ensued.

Several men went missing after they visited Coeur d'Alene for a night on the town. Bodies are still being unearthed here and there, their identities unknown.

The last surviving brothels in Idaho were located in Wallace. There were a half dozen bordellos in town, and no one seemed to mind. That was until the mid-1980s, when over 150 FBI (Federal Bureau of Investigations) rolled into Wallace and raided fifty-eight bars and establishments.

A local rumor says that the FBI wasn't even in Wallace for prostitution; it was just assumed, and the working girls took to running as fast as they could go. Perhaps the truth will never be known. One thing is for sure, the FBI left town with a lot of incriminating evidence.

CONCLUSION

The beautiful city of Coeur d'Alene began as a stormy ride of excitement, struggle, murders and mayhem created by all the people who desired to live and work there. Through ongoing hardships, they continued to strive to improve the city, increase the town's revenue and make it desirable to both tourists and newcomers alike.

Early Coeur d'Alene was a strange mix of immigrants, railroad and miner workers, gold rush junkies, prostitutes, bootleggers, scandalous government officials, ruthless cowboys and bandits, cold-blooded killers and more.

I hope this book has offered you an inside look at the interesting early life of Coeur d'Alene, its nearby towns and all its colorful characters from the past. I pray that when you visit the city or walk the streets there, you will think of these old-timers and their hardships, sacrifices, faith and visions.

If you pass by any of the original Coeur d'Alene buildings from yesteryear, please pause for a moment or two and remember the people who built them and why. If you find yourself at the corner of some of these streets, pay your respects to the individuals who lost their lives in those exact spots one hundred years ago.

And take a few moments to relish in Coeur d'Alene's fantastic beauty and breathe in the cool, fresh air blowing off the nearby water.

BIBLIOGRAPHY

Articles

Camas Prairie Chronicle. "Shooting Scare in Mullan." April 19, 1901.

Coeur d'Alene Evening Press. "Is Dead Man William Ingstrom?" May 24, 1909.

———. "Lake Revels Foul Murder." May 22, 1908.

Coeur d'Alene Press. "Early Coeur d'Alene and Kootenai County." October 23, 1897; June 1, 1901; April 5, 1902; April 27, 1909.

———. "Floater Found." April 8, 1907; May 22 and 27, 1907; July 25, 1907; July 27, 1909.

———. "Horse Stealing." May 18, 1909.

———. "John Metcalf Turns Gun on Himself." May 27. 1907.

———. "Police Land Burglar." May 27, 1907.

———. "Quinn Murder." April 25, 1907.

———. "Shooting Scare in Mullan." April 20, 1901.

Daily Star Mirror. "Doc Cain Murder." August 23, 1915.

DeArment, R.K. "Two-Gun' Hart: The Prohibition Cowboy." Historynet. https://www.historynet.com/two-gun-hart-the-prohibition-cowboy.htm.

Duluth Labor World. "John Macki Interview." July 27, 1907.

Grangeville Globe. "Chinamen Hanged at Pierce." September 11, 1913.

Lewiston Evening Teller. "Quinn Murder." September 20, 1907.

Lewiston Teller. "Sinking Steamer on Coeur d'Alene River." April 14, 1887.

Mailey/Rice Murder

Coeur d'Alene Press, December 7, 1901.
Emmett Index, December 5, 1900.
Lewiston Daily Teller, January 4 and 5, 1901.
Payette Independent, October 4, 1900.
Weiser Signal, December 6, 1900.

Owen Perry's Murder

Alaskan Citizen, October 9, 1911.
Kendrick Gazette, October 13, 1911.

Rossi Murder Trial

Evening Capital News, October 6, 13 and 15; December 5, 1916.

Books

Berg, Captain Carl, Lieutenant Ron Hotchkiss and Sergeant Christie Wood. *The Written History of the Coeur d'Alene Police Department 1887–2012*. Coeur d'Alene, ID: Coeur d'Alene Police Department, 2011. https://www.cdaid.org/files/police/CDAPD_History_Written.pdf.
Brainard, Wendell. *Golden History Tales from Idaho's Coeur d'Alene Mining District*. Wallace, ID: Kingsbury Foundation, 1990.
Hamilton, Ladd. *This Bloody Deed: The Magruder Incident*. First published in 1994. Pullman: Washington State University Press, 2013.
Roizen, Ron. *The Rossi Murder*. N.p.: Wallace, ID: self-published, 2021.

Websites

Ancestry. www.ancestry.com.
Enjoy Coeur d'Alene. www.enjoycoeurdalene.com.

Find a Grave. www.findagrave.com.
History Link. www.historylink.org.
Library of Congress. www.libraryofcongress.org.
National Archives and Records Administration. www.nationalarchives.org.
Rozien. www.roizen.com.
Wikimedia. www.wikimedia.org.
Wikipedia. www.wikipedia.org.

Miscellaneous

Alcohol Problems and Solutions. "Prohibition in Idaho Caused Serious Problems." https://www.alcoholproblemsandsolutions.org/prohibition-in-idaho/.

Coeur d'Alene Press. "Coeur d'Alene: 100 Years." 1987.

Editors of Encyclopedia Britannica. "Pinkerton National Detective Agency." *Encyclopedia Britannica*, September 25, 2017. www.britannica.com.

Garrison, Mary. "Idaho's submarine Fleet." Spokane Historical. https://spokanehistorical.org/items/show/589.

Hurt, Paul (professor), and Katherine Aiken. History 422, lecture 11. Washington State University, n.d.

Idaho State Archives. AR 201 Kootenai County. Box: 20155069, Civil–Criminal Case Files, A-COB, 1882–1952. Folder: *State of Idaho v. Dr. R.J. Alcorn, AKA A.J. Alcorn.*

———. AR 201 Kootenai County. Box: 20155072, Civil–Criminal Case Files, K MA, 1880-1952. Folder: *State of Idaho v. LaFenirer.*

———. AR 201 Kootenai County. Box: 20155070, Civil–Criminal Case Files, COL-GO, 1882–1952. Folder: *State of Idaho v. N.H. Coryell.*

Idaho State Historical Society. "Inmates of the Idaho Penitentiary 1864–1947." Public archives and research, 2008.

Jennifer. "Not Many People Know there's an Eerily Beautiful Shipwreck Hiding Right Here in Idaho." Only in Your State, April 23, 2017. https://www.onlyinyourstate.com/idaho/lake-shipwreck-id/.

Lake Coeur d'Alene Cruises. "What's Below the Surface—A Glimpse at the History of Sunken Ships in the Northwest." May 6, 2016. https://www.cdacruises.com/2016/05/06/whats-below-the-surface-a-glimpse-at-the-history-of-sunken-ships-in-the-northwest/.

Lewiston Teller, April 4, 1887.

Redfern, Nick. "Paddler, the Submarine Monster." Mysterious Universe, March 18, 2015. https://mysteriousuniverse.org/2015/03/paddler-the-submarine-monster/.

South Fork Companion. "1887 Capsized *Spokane*." https://sfcompanion.blogspot.com/2020/04/steamer-accident-kills-five-on-coeur-d.html.

Wikipedia. "Steamboats on Lake Coeur d'Alene." www.wikipedia.com.

John Macki Murder

Powell, Cynthia S. "Beyond Molly b'Damn: Prostitutes in the Coeur d'Alene's 1880–1911." Master's thesis, Central Washington University, 1994.

Putman, E. "The Prohibition Movement in Idaho 1863–1934." PhD diss., University of Idaho, 1979.

Raye, Janet. "We Never Forget." *Hellraisers Journal*, 2017.

Roizen, Ron. "The Hill Beachy Project." www.roizen.com.

Smith, Robert Wayne. "The Coeur d'Alene Mining War of 1892." Office of Publications by Oregon State University Press, 1961. www.osupress.oregonstate.edu.

Sunken Ore

Hentges, Katherine. "The Sunken Ore of Lake Coeur d'Alene." Spokane Historical. https://spokanehistorical.org/items/show/883.

Lake Coeur d'Alene. "Recent updates from Kootenai County Parks & Waterways." May 21, 2020. https://www.lakecoeurdalene.com/blog/.

Major Wilkins. "Fort Sherman, Idaho." Reference notebooks of a local historian. Coeur d'Alene Library, 1993.

Wikipedia. "1899 Coeur d'Alene Labor Confrontation." www.en.wikipedia.org.

Wolff, Fritz E. "Industrial Espionage 1890s Style: Undercover Agents in the Coeur d'Alene Mining District." https://www.mininghistoryassociation.org/Journal/MHJ-v9-2002-Wolff.pdf.

Zimmerman, Caila. "Prostitution in the Mining Community of Wallace, Idaho." University of Idaho, *Intermountain Histories*. https://www.intermountainhistories.org/items/show/111.

ABOUT THE AUTHOR

Originally from upstate New York, Deborah Cuyle loves everything about small towns and their history. Her passions include local history, animals, museums, hiking and horseback riding. She, her husband and her son remodeled a historic house in Wallace, Idaho, and are currently remodeling a crumbling 1883 mansion in Milbank, South Dakota. She has written:

- *Ghosts of Coeur d'Alene and the Silver Valley* (ID)
- *Murder & Mayhem in Coeur d'Alene and the Silver Valley* (ID)
- *Wicked Coeur d'Alene* (ID)
- *Ghosts and Legends of Spokane* (WA)
- *Wicked Spokane* (WA)
- *Ghosts of Leavenworth and the Cascade Foothills* (WA)
- *Haunted Snohomish* (WA)
- *Ghostly Tales of Snohomish* (WA, young adult version)
- *Ghostly Tales of the Pacific Northwest* (young adult version)
- *Haunted Everett* (WA)
- *The 1910 Wellington Disaster* (WA)
- *Images of Cannon Beach* (OR)
- *Kidding Around Portland* (OR)

Keep an eye out for her next books: *Murder & Mayhem in Spokane* and *Haunted Anaconda*!